Letters
from God
for Women

Presented to:

With Much
Love

Presented by:

Date:

Letters *from* God *for* WOMEN

God's Faithful Promises for You

HARVEST HOUSE PUBLISHERS

EUGENE, OREGON

Letters from God for Women

ISBN 0-7369-1257-6
Copyright © 2004 by GRQ Ink, Inc.

Published by Harvest House Publishers
Eugene, OR 97402
www.harvesthousepublishers.com

Developed by GRQ Ink, Inc.
Manuscript written by Diane Noble
Cover and text design by Whisner Design Group
Composition by Educational Publishing Concepts, Inc.

Printed in China.   05 06 07 08 09 10 / RDS / 7 6 5 4 3

A Letter from God

Beloved,

I watch your hours fill to overflowing with the busy details of your life. I see your concern for your family and friends. So many depend on you, dear one, making your responsibilities seem overwhelming and, at times, your weariness soul-deep.

Did you know that I created you to draw strength from My presence? Did you know that I delight in your knowledge of Me? I long to refresh you; I long to open My heart to you.

So come to Me. Learn of Me. You will find rest for your soul, My daughter, and peace beyond understanding. Come to the still waters of My presence and draw joyously from the wellspring of My riches.

Waiting for you,

Your Heavenly Father

Come to me. Get away with me and you'll recover your life. I'll show you how to take a real rest. Walk with me and work with me—watch how I do it. Learn the unforced rhythms of grace. I won't lay anything heavy or ill-fitting on you. Keep company with me and you'll learn to live freely and lightly.

MATTHEW 11:28-30 THE MESSAGE

Contents

Letters *from* God *for* WOMEN

COME TO THE WATERS

I want to quench your thirst.

Dear One,

Just as the sun-scorched ground longs for rain, you long for refreshment; your heart hungers to be satisfied. Do you know that I am here, waiting to quench your thirst and satisfy your hunger forever?

You can find nothing more satisfying than what I offer you, and yet that which I give you is priceless and without cost.

Come to My waters. Drink deeply from My presence. Taste the sweetness of My mercy, peace, and joy. Find rest and refreshment for your spirit; it costs you nothing. I am the Spring whose waters never fail.

Waiting for you,

The One Who Loves You

> The Lord will guide you continually,
> And satisfy your soul in drought,
> And strengthen your bones;
> You shall be like a watered garden,
> And like a spring of water,
> whose waters do not fail.
>
> ISAIAH 58:11 NKJV

Return to your rest, O my soul,
For the Lord has dealt
bountifully with you.
PSALM 116:7 NASB

Ho, everyone who thirsts,
come to the waters;
and you that have no money,
come, buy and eat!
Come, buy wine and milk
without money and without price.
Why do you spend your money
for that which is not bread,
and your labor for that which
does not satisfy?
Listen carefully to me, and eat what is good,
and delight yourselves in rich food.
ISAIAH 55:1-2 NRSV

It is useless for you to work so hard
from early morning until late at night,
anxiously working for food to eat;
for God gives rest to his loved ones.
PSALM 127:2 NLT

Live under the protection of God Most High
and stay in the shadow of God All-Powerful.
PSALM 91:1 CEV

Rest and Refreshment

Rest and Refreshment

*I am Alpha and Omega, the beginning and the
end. I will give unto him that is athirst of the
fountain of the water of life freely.*
REVELATION 21:6

Blessed are those who trust in the LORD and have
made the LORD their hope and confidence. They
are like trees planted along a riverbank, with
roots that reach deep into the water. Such trees
are not bothered by the heat or worried by long
months of drought. Their leaves stay green, and
they go right on producing delicious fruit.
JEREMIAH 17:7-8 NLT

They are like trees growing beside a stream,
trees that produce fruit in season
and always have leaves.
PSALM 1:3 CEV

He shall come down like rain upon the mown
grass: as showers that water the earth.
PSALM 72:6

He makes me lie down in green pastures.
He leads me beside peaceful waters.
PSALM 23:2 GOD'S WORD

I stretched out my hands to you,
as thirsty for you as a desert thirsty for rain.
PSALM 143:6 THE MESSAGE

The meek shall eat and be satisfied: they
shall praise the LORD that seek him: your
heart shall live for ever.

PSALM 22:26

I truly am thirsty for you, my God.
In my heart, I am thirsty for you,
the living God.
When will I see your face?

PSALM 42:1-2 CEV

"Come!" say the Spirit and the Bride.
Whoever hears, echo, "Come!"
Is anyone thirsty? Come!
All who will, come and drink,
Drink freely of the
Water of Life!

REVELATION 22:17 THE MESSAGE

O God, you are my God;
I earnestly search for you.
My soul thirsts for you;
my whole body longs for you
in this parched and weary land where
there is no water.

PSALM 63:1 NLT

Come to
the Waters

My Gifts for You

You cannot fathom the riches I have for you.

My Daughter,

Just as an earthly father longs to shower his beloved child with gifts, how much more do I desire to give you! I delight in you, beloved, and long to bless you with riches more abundant than you can imagine.

Lift your head and know that I bestow My honor and favor upon you. Breathe in My peace, and feel My strength lift you. Let My joy bubble from deep within your heart. These are all My gifts, just as My guidance, faithfulness, might, and compassion are all yours as well.

Each day My riches await your discovery. Open your arms, open your heart, and accept them, My child. They are yours.

With blessings abundant,

Your Heavenly Father

Riches and honor are with me, enduring wealth and prosperity. My fruit is better than gold, even fine gold, and my yield than choice silver.

PROVERBS 8:18-19 NRSV

*But to each one of us grace
was given according to the
measure of Christ's gift.*
EPHESIANS 4:7 NKJV

His divine power has given us everything
needed for life and godliness, through the
knowledge of him who called us by his own
glory and goodness.
2 PETER 1:3 NRSV

The hearing ear, and the seeing eye,
The LORD hath made even both of them.
PROVERBS 20:12

I am leaving you with a gift—peace of mind
and heart. And the peace I give isn't like the
peace the world gives.
So don't be troubled or afraid.
JOHN 14:27 NLT

Be glad, O people of Zion, rejoice in the
LORD your God, for he has given you the
autumn rains in righteousness.
He sends you abundant showers, both
autumn and spring rains, as before.
JOEL 2:23 NIV

God's Gifts

I WILL NEVER LEAVE YOU

I walk beside you.

My Own,

The concerns of daily life often trouble your heart. You think that you are alone in your worries and must handle everything by yourself. I long for you to know that I walk beside you through every dark valley and with every halting step you take as you struggle to keep going. I long for you to know that when you stumble or feel weary, I am there.

I will never abandon you, dear one! I am with you, waiting for you to let Me help you through every troubling moment of every circumstance in your life. Lean on Me, My daughter, and know that My promise to be with you will last through all eternity.

With deepest love,

The One Who Will Never Forsake You

> The Rock! His work is perfect,
> For all His ways are just;
> A God of faithfulness and without injustice,
> Righteous and upright is He.
> DEUTERONOMY 32:4 NASB

Those who know your name will
trust in you, for you, LORD,
have never forsaken those
who seek you.
PSALM 9:10 NIV

I will lead the blind by a road they do not know,
by paths they have not known I will guide them.
I will turn the darkness before them into light,
the rough places into level ground.
These are the things I will do,
and I will not forsake them.
ISAIAH 42:16 NRSV

The mountains shall depart, and the hills be
removed; but my kindness shall not depart from
thee, neither shall the covenant of my peace be
removed, saith the LORD that hath
mercy on thee.
ISAIAH 54:10

I will betroth you to Me forever;
Yes, I will betroth you to Me in righteousness
and in justice,
In lovingkindness and in compassion,
And I will betroth you to Me in faithfulness.
Then you will know the LORD.
HOSEA 2:19-20 NASB

Faithfulness

I KNOW YOUR HEART

I can see the inner stirrings of your soul.

My Beloved,

A true friend listens when you hurt, rejoices when you enjoy good news, and gathers you into her arms when you grieve. Sometimes, however, even your closest friend cannot fully understand what you are going through. And sometimes, your sorrows and longings may be too private to share.

My daughter, I have wonderful news! I know and understand every whispered dream, every emotional distress, and every joyful dance of your heart. I know and understand every one of your innermost longings.

Because I made you, I *know* you. This knowledge gives Me the most intimate understanding possible. Pour out your heart to Me. I am waiting and listening, even now.

In total love,

The One Who Knows and Understands

All my longings lie open before you, O LORD;
my sighing is not hidden from you.
PSALM 38:9 NIV

*Great is our Lord,
and of great power:
his understanding
is infinite.*
PSALM 147:5

O LORD, you have examined my heart
and know everything about me.
You know when I sit down or stand up.
You know my every thought when far away.
You chart the path ahead of me
and tell me where to stop and rest.
Every moment you know where I am.
You know what I am going to say
even before I say it, LORD.
You both precede and follow me.
You place your hand of blessing on my head.
Such knowledge is too wonderful for me,
too great for me to know!
PSALM 139:1-6 NLT

From the place of His dwelling He looks
On all the inhabitants of the earth;
He fashions their hearts individually,
He considers all their works.
PSALM 33:14-15 NKJV

Understanding

Understanding

*He cutteth out rivers among the rocks; and his eye
seeth every precious thing.*

JOB 28:10

She gave this name to the LORD who spoke to her:
"You are the God who sees me," for she said, "I
have now seen the One who sees me."

GENESIS 16:13 NIV

Look up into the heavens. Who created all the
stars? He brings them out one after another, calling
each by its name. And He counts them to see that
none are lost or have strayed away.

How can you say the LORD does not see your
troubles? How can you say God refuses to hear
your case? Have you never heard or understood?
Don't you know that the LORD is the everlasting
God, the Creator of all the earth? He never grows
faint or weary. No one can measure the
depths of his understanding.

ISAIAH 40:26-28 NLT

In him we have redemption through his blood, the
forgiveness of our trespasses, according to the
riches of his grace that he lavished on us. With all
wisdom and insight he has made known to us the
mystery of his will, according to his good pleasure
that he set forth in Christ.

EPHESIANS 1:7-9 NRSV

Hear them in heaven, where you live.
Forgive them, and take action.
Give each person the proper reply.
(You know what is in their hearts,
because you alone know what is in the
hearts of all people.)

1 KINGS 8:39 GOD'S WORD

He made the earth by his power,
and he preserves it by his wisdom.
He has stretched out the heavens
by his understanding.

JEREMIAH 51:15 NLT

Now we see things imperfectly as in a poor
mirror, but then we will see everything with
perfect clarity. All that I know now is partial
and incomplete, but then I will know
everything completely,
just as God knows me now.

1 CORINTHIANS 13:12 NLT

I, the LORD, search minds and test hearts.
I will reward each person
for what he has done.
I will reward him for the
results of his actions.

JEREMIAH 17:10 GOD'S WORD

I Know
Your Heart

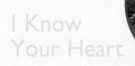

19

YOUR BEAUTY IN ME

I am making you into My image.

My Daughter,

Did you know that I created you to be like no one else on earth? The combination of your genes, cells, muscle fibers, and talents are unique. My child, I even designed your DNA blueprint before the beginning of time! There is no one else, anywhere, the same as you.

Your design includes the imprint of My image in your heart. Think of it! I created you to reflect My glory, My truth, My compassion, My peace, My love—*all* of who I am. Open your heart to consciously become more like Me each day, precious one. This beauty will last forever.

Transforming you,

Your Creator

> One thing I ask of the LORD,
> this is what I seek:
> that I may dwell in the house of the LORD
> all the days of my life,
> to gaze upon the beauty of the LORD
> and to seek him in his temple.
> PSALM 27:4 NIV

*Charm is deceptive, and
beauty does not last; but a
woman who fears the LORD
will be greatly praised.*
PROVERBS 31:30 NLT

Do not let your adornment be *merely*
outward—arranging the hair, wearing gold, or
putting on *fine* apparel—rather *let it be* the
hidden person of the heart, with the
incorruptible *beauty* of a gentle and quiet spirit,
which is very precious in the sight of God.
1 PETER 3:3-4 NKJV

I will make your battlements of rubies,
your gates of sparkling jewels,
and all your walls of precious stones.
ISAIAH 54:12 NIV

Let the beauty of the LORD our God be upon us:
and establish thou the work of our hands upon
us; yea, the work of our hands establish thou it.
PSALM 90:17

God gives such beauty to everything that grows
in the fields, even though it is here today and
thrown into a fire tomorrow. Won't he do even
more for you? You have such little faith!
LUKE 12:28 CEV

Self-Worth

MY LIGHT IN YOUR DARKNESS

The light of My countenance can fill you.

My Own,

Sometimes I see that anxieties, doubts, and discouragement cast shadows of darkness across your path. These are not from Me, beloved, but from the enemy who would have you believe his darkness is greater than My light. I have a glorious light for you, My child—keep your eyes on Me!

When you encounter darkness, My precious daughter, hold on to the truth! All that I am is yours. If you but ask, My tender mercies and My compassion will flood your soul. Let Me turn your discouragement to joy, your doubts to faith, your anxieties to trust, your hopelessness to hope, and your darkness to light.

With mercy,

The Father of Lights

With thee *is* the fountain of life:
in thy light shall we see light.
PSALM 36:9

*His life is the light that shines
through the darkness —
and the darkness can never
extinguish it.*
JOHN 1:4-5 TLB

The LORD is my light and my salvation—
so why should I be afraid?
The LORD protects me from danger—
so why should I tremble?
PSALM 27:1 NLT

Those who walked in the dark
have seen a bright light.
And it shines upon everyone
who lives in the land
of darkest shadows.
ISAIAH 9:2 CEV

I will be glad and rejoice in Your mercy,
For You have considered my trouble;
You have known my soul in adversities.
PSALM 31:7 NKJV

Let us therefore draw near with confidence
to the throne of grace, that we may receive
mercy and may find grace
to help in time of need.
HEBREWS 4:16 NASB

Mercy of God

Mercy of God

*For once you were darkness, but now in the Lord
you are light. Live as children of light — for the
fruit of the light is found in all that is good and
right and true.*

EPHESIANS 5:8-9 NRSV

God said, "Let there be light," and there was light.
God saw that the light was good, and he separated
the light from the darkness.

GENESIS 1:3-4 NIV

You would forget *your* trouble,
As waters that have passed by, you would
remember *it*.
Your life would be brighter than noonday;
Darkness would be like the morning.

JOB 11:16-17 NASB

You, LORD, are the light that keeps me safe.
I am not afraid of anyone.
You protect me, and I have no fears.

PSALM 27:1 CEV

Jesus said to the people, "I am the light of the
world. If you follow me, you won't be stumbling
through the darkness, because you will have the
light that leads to life."

JOHN 8:12 NLT

You have changed my sobbing into dancing.
You have removed my sackcloth and clothed Me
with joy so that my soul may praise you with
music and not be silent.
O Lord my God, I will give thanks to
you forever.

PSALM 30:11-12 GOD'S WORD

The Lord is our God, and he has given us light!
Start the celebration!
March with palm branches all the way
to the altar.

PSALM 118:27 CEV

Your sun will never set again,
and your moon will wane no more;
the Lord will be your everlasting light,
and your days of sorrow will end.

ISAIAH 60:20 NIV

Then shall thy light break forth as the morning,
and thine health shall spring forth speedily: and
thy righteousness shall go before thee; the glory
of the Lord shall be thy rereward.

ISAIAH 58:8

My Light in
Your Darkness

Listen for My Voice

My voice can change your heart.

My Beloved,

You raise your eyes to observe My beauty in a sunset; you marvel at My touch in a gentle breeze. You delight in the sounds of My creation—a baby's first laugh, a robin's song, or a flutter of leaves on a fall day. You stand in awe at the majesty of My voice when the ocean waves crash or thunder rolls.

But I speak to you alone, My child, in the quiet of your heart. Draw near to Me. Listen for My whisper, still and small, in the depths of your soul. Listen for My words of comfort and joy and wisdom and strength. Quiet yourself before Me, My daughter. Even now, I speak.

With love,

Your Heavenly Father

> My sheep know my voice, and I know them. They follow me.
> JOHN 10:27 CEV

The watchman opens the gate for him, and the sheep listen to his voice. He calls his own sheep by name and leads them out.
JOHN 10:3 NIV

The LORD is our God, and we are his people, the sheep he takes care of in his own pasture. Listen to God's voice today!
PSALM 95:7 CEV

He said, "Go out, and stand on the mountain before the LORD." And behold, the LORD passed by, and a great and strong wind tore into the mountains and broke the rocks in pieces before the LORD, *but* the LORD *was* not in the wind; and after the wind an earthquake, *but* the LORD *was* not in the earthquake; and after the earthquake a fire, *but* the LORD *was* not in the fire; and after the fire a still small voice.
1 KINGS 19:11-12 NKJV

The voice of the LORD is over the waters;
the God of glory thunders,
the LORD, over mighty waters.
The voice of the LORD is powerful;
the voice of the LORD is full of majesty.
PSALM 29:3-4 NRSV

Hearing God

LEAN INTO MY ARMS

I am always here.

My Dearest Daughter,

I see your need for someone to hold you, to listen to you, to take delight in you, and to feed and comfort you. Just as a nursing mother provides life-giving food to her child, so can I give spiritual nourishment to you!

In your fast-paced and often hectic world, and even as you care for so many others, you can forget I am near. I long to gather you close and provide the soul-nourishment you need.

Come to Me, beloved, in the quiet of dawn or in the silence of the night. Lean on Me throughout your day. You will find comfort in My arms. I am never too busy for you.

Waiting for you,

The One Who Waits to Nourish and Refresh

As one whom his mother comforts,
So I will comfort you.
ISAIAH 66:13 NKJV

*I will refresh the weary
and satisfy the faint.*
JEREMIAH 31:25 NIV

I have stilled and quieted myself, just as a small
child is quiet with its mother. Yes, like a small
child is my soul within me.
PSALM 131:2 NLT

Sing, O heavens; and be joyful, O earth; and
break forth into singing, O mountains: for the
LORD hath comforted his people, and will have
mercy upon his afflicted.
ISAIAH 49:13

The LORD is near to everyone
who prays to him,
to every faithful person who prays to him.
PSALM 145:18 GOD'S WORD

O my people in Jerusalem, you shall weep no
more, for he will surely be gracious to you at
the sound of your cry. He will answer you.
ISAIAH 30:19 TLB

Comfort

Comfort

Praise be to the God and Father of our Lord Jesus Christ, the Father of compassion and the God of all comfort, who comforts us in all our troubles, so that we can comfort those in any trouble with the comfort we ourselves have received from God. For just as the sufferings of Christ flow over into our lives, so also through Christ our comfort overflows.
2 CORINTHIANS 1:3-5 NIV

Don't be troubled. Believe in God,
and believe in me.
JOHN 14:1 GOD'S WORD

I will pray the Father, and he shall give you another Comforter, that he may abide with you for ever; *Even* the Spirit of truth; whom the world cannot receive, because it seeth him not, neither knoweth him: but ye know him; for he dwelleth with you, and shall be in you.
JOHN 14:16-17

You keep track of all my sorrows.
You have collected all my tears in your bottle.
You have recorded each one in your book.
PSALM 56:8 NLT

God is our refuge and strength,
a very present help in trouble.
PSALM 46:1

Even though I walk through the darkest
valley, I fear no evil;
for you are with me;
your rod and your staff—
they comfort me.

PSALM 23:4 NRSV

Like infants at the breast, drink deep of
God's pure kindness. Then you'll grow up
mature and whole in God.

I PETER 2:2-3 THE MESSAGE

Give your burdens to the LORD,
and he will take care of you.
He will not permit the godly to slip and fall.

PSALM 55:22 NLT

Unless the LORD *had been* my help, My soul
had almost dwelt in silence.
When I said, My foot slippeth; thy mercy,
O LORD, held me up. In the multitude of my
thoughts within me thy comforts
delight my soul.

PSALM 94:17-19

Lean into
My Arms

A WOMAN'S BUSY WORLD

Put Me first in your life.

Dear One,

Your busy days, with responsibilities in the workplace as well as in your home, can pull your attention a dozen different ways. My heart aches when I see you struggle with financial worries or relationships that need mending. Too often you try to fix everything yourself, setting ever-changing priorities that cannot stand up to the constant demands on your time. Defeat and fatigue set in, and you are robbed of My peace and joy.

Beloved child—and I say this gently—put your relationship with Me before all else. I care about your problems and will help you figure out solutions. When I am first in your life, everything else will fall into place.

With so much to give,

The One Who Loves You

> People who don't know God and the way he works fuss over these things, but you know both God and how he works. Steep your life in God-reality, God-initiative, God-provisions. Don't worry about missing out. You'll find all your everyday human concerns will be met.
> MATTHEW 6:32-33 THE MESSAGE

*I want you to understand
what really matters, so
that you may live pure and
blameless lives until
Christ returns.*

PHILIPPIANS 1:10 NLT

My child, do not forget my teaching,
but let your heart keep my commandments;
for length of days and years of life
and abundant welfare they will give you.

PROVERBS 3:1-2 NRSV

God gives some people the ability to enjoy the
wealth and property he gives them, as well as the
ability to accept their state in life and enjoy their
work. They do not worry about how short life is,
because God keeps them busy with
what they love to do.

ECCLESIASTES 5:19-20 NCV

You don't know what will happen tomorrow.
What is life? You are a mist that is seen for a
moment and then disappears. Instead, you should
say, "If the Lord wants us to, we will live and
carry out our plans."

JAMES 4:14-15 GOD'S WORD

Priorities

THE TREE IN YOUR HEART'S GARDEN

I am the Gardener who tends your heart.

My Own,

Consider how your life is like a garden—bursting with the potential to produce rich and wonderful fruit. Just as seeds are planted in the ground, so seeds of faith are planted in your heart. When the seedlings sprout, their roots and tender leaves need sunlight and water. The soil must be tended in preparation for growth.

Trust Me to be the Gardener who will lovingly nurture your spirit and your spiritual growth. Let Me work in your heart, tending to every part of your life. You will rejoice in the beautiful, lasting fruit that your spirit will produce.

With tender care,

Your Heart's Gardener

May you always be filled with the fruit of your salvation—those good things that are produced in your life by Jesus Christ—for this will bring much glory and praise to God.
PHILIPPIANS 1:11 NLT

I am like a large olive tree in God's house. I trust the mercy of God forever and ever.

PSALM 52:8 GOD'S WORD

BLESSINGS ON ALL who reverence and trust the Lord—on all who obey him! Their reward shall be prosperity and happiness. Your wife shall be contented in your home. And look at all those children! There they sit around the dinner table as vigorous and healthy as young olive trees. That is God's reward to those who reverence and trust him.

PSALM 128:1-4 TLB

They are strong, like a tree planted by a river. The tree produces fruit in season, and its leaves don't die. Everything they do will succeed.

PSALM 1:3 NCV

For as the earth bringeth forth her bud, and as the garden causeth the things that are sown in it to spring forth; so the Lord GOD will cause righteousness and praise to spring forth before all the nations.

ISAIAH 61:11

Fruitfulness

BRING MY LOVE TO ANOTHER'S HEART

My love changes lives.

Precious One,

Others can know Me through your love. This kind of compassion for others is not always easy, however. It is a love without condition. It includes the unlovely and the unlovable, those who have hurt you through words or deeds, and those who live differently from you. Such love, filled with forgiveness and grace, is without end.

This kind of love is impossible without Me. Ask for My help in loving those that you bring before me. Let them see My love in your eyes and in the works of your hands. Their lives—and yours—will be transformed.

With complete love,

Your Heavenly Father

No one has ever seen God. But if we love each other, God lives in us, and his love has been brought to full expression through us.

1 JOHN 4:12 NLT

*Make every effort to keep
the unity of the Spirit
through the bond of peace.*
EPHESIANS 4:3 NIV

Do all these things; but most important, love
each other. Love is what holds you all together
in perfect unity.
COLOSSIANS 3:14 NCV

You obeyed the truth, and your souls were made
pure. Now you sincerely love each other. But
you must keep on loving with all your heart.
1 PETER 1:22 CEV

This is the message that ye heard from the
beginning, that we should love one another.
1 JOHN 3:11

Beloved, let us love one another, because love is
from God; everyone who loves is
born of God and knows God.
1 JOHN 4:7 NRSV

Don't just pretend that you love others.
Really love them.
ROMANS 12:9 NLT

Loving Others

I Am with You

I will never leave you.

Dear One,

I am near even when you are not aware of My presence. Nothing happens that I don't know about it. I hear every word spoken to you, harsh or kind. I share every circumstance, hurtful or joyful. I feel every struggle, every longing, and every triumph. I treasure you.

I love you as if you were the only one in the world to love! I walk beside you through your days. I watch over you as you sleep. I am near when you pray, when you weep, and when you laugh with joy. Reach out and take My hand, beloved. I will never leave you.

Your best Friend,

The Lord Your God

My dwelling place will be with them; I will be their God, and they will be my people.

EZEKIEL 37:27 NIV

I have inscribed you on the palms of My hands; Your walls are continually before Me.
ISAIAH 49:16 NKJV

Can a woman forget her nursing child?
Will she have no compassion
on the child from her womb?
Although mothers may forget,
I will not forget you.
ISAIAH 49:15 GOD'S WORD

He has brought you back as his friends. He has
done this through his death on the cross in his
own human body. As a result, he has brought
you into the very presence of God, and you
are holy and blameless as you stand before him
without a single fault.
COLOSSIANS 1:22 NLT

Where could I go to escape
from your Spirit or from your sight?
If I were to climb up to the highest heavens,
you would be there.
If I were to dig down to the world of the dead
you would also be there.
PSALM 139:7-8 CEV

Presence of God

Presence of God

*"Do not be afraid of them, for I am with you and
will rescue you," declares the Lord.*
JEREMIAH 1:8 NIV

Jacob woke up from his sleep and exclaimed,
"Certainly, the LORD is in this place,
and I didn't know it!"
GENESIS 28:16 GOD'S WORD

I am convinced that nothing can ever separate us
from his love. Death can't, and life can't. The angels
can't, and the demons can't. Our fears for today,
our worries about tomorrow, and even the powers
of hell can't keep God's love away.
ROMANS 8:38 NLT

Sing and rejoice, O daughter of Zion: for, lo, I come,
and I will dwell in the midst of thee, saith the LORD.
ZECHARIAH 2:10

The Lord is close to those whose hearts are
breaking; he rescues those who are
humbly sorry for their sins.
PSALM 34:18 TLB

Thus says the high and lofty one
who inhabits eternity, whose name is Holy:
I dwell in the high and holy place,
and also with those who are contrite and
humble in spirit,
to revive the spirit of the humble,
and to revive the heart of the contrite.

ISAIAH 57:15 NRSV

If we obey God's commandments, we will
stay one in our hearts with him, and he will
stay one with us. The Spirit that he has given
us is proof that we are one with him.

1 JOHN 3:24 CEV

Do you not know that you are the temple of
God and *that* the Spirit of God
dwells in you?

1 CORINTHIANS 3:16 NKJV

"Am I a God who is only in one place?" asks
the LORD. "Do they think I cannot see what
they are doing? Can anyone hide from me?
Am I not everywhere in all the heavens and
earth?" asks the LORD.

JEREMIAH 23:23-24 NLT

I Am with You

Just As You Are, My Child!

I love you just as you are.

My Daughter,

Sometimes I see you struggling beneath a burden that I could carry for you. But you think yourself unworthy of My help and do not turn to Me. It breaks My heart, dear one, to see you judge yourself so harshly. I long for you to know that you stand beautiful and beloved in My sight.

You cannot earn My favor. It is already yours—and in greater abundance than you can imagine! Come into My arms, and let Me fill your heart with My mercy, forgiveness, and grace. Listen to My voice as I rejoice over you. Can you imagine such love? It is yours, beloved.

With grace beyond measure,

The One Who Loves You

I will tell of the LORD's unfailing love. I will praise the LORD for all he has done. I will rejoice in his great goodness to Israel, which he has granted according to his mercy and love.

ISAIAH 63:7 NLT

You gave me life and showed me kindness, and in your providence watched over my spirit.

JOB 10:12 NIV

"Master, how can I, your servant, talk with you? My strength is gone, and it is hard for me to breathe." The one who looked like a man touched me again and gave me strength. He said, "Daniel, don't be afraid. God loves you very much. Peace be with you. Be strong now; be courageous."

DANIEL 10:17-19 NCV

I will greatly rejoice in the LORD, my soul shall be joyful in my God; for he hath clothed me with the garments of salvation, he hath covered me with the robe of righteousness, as a bridegroom decketh *himself* with ornaments, and as a bride adorneth *herself* with her jewels.

ISAIAH 61:10

He brought me forth also into a large place; he delivered me because he delighted in me.

PSALM 18:19

Acceptance

Acceptance

There is no fear in love. But perfect love drives out fear, because fear has to do with punishment. The one who fears is not made perfect in love.
1 JOHN 4:18 NIV

Because of Christ and our faith in him, we can now come fearlessly into God's presence, assured of his glad welcome.
EPHESIANS 3:12 NLT

Now that we have God's approval by faith, we have peace with God because of what our Lord Jesus Christ has done. Through Christ we can approach God and stand in his favor.
ROMANS 5:1-2 GOD'S WORD

His joy is in those who reverence him, those who expect him to be loving and kind.
PSALM 147:11 TLB

How blessed is God! And what a blessing he is! He's the Father of our Master, Jesus Christ, and takes us to the high places of blessing in him.
EPHESIANS 1:3 THE MESSAGE

Jehovah enjoys his people;
he will save the humble.
PSALM 149:4 TLB

His favor is with everyone who has an
undying love for our Lord Jesus Christ.

EPHESIANS 6:24 GOD'S WORD

Answer me, O LORD, out of the goodness of
your love; in your great mercy turn to me.

PSALM 69:16 NIV

Long ago, even before he made the world,
God loved us and chose us in Christ to be
holy and without fault in his eyes. His
unchanging plan has always been to adopt us
into his own family by bringing us to himself
through Jesus Christ. And this gave him
great pleasure.

EPHESIANS 1:4-5 NLT

He calls his friends and neighbors together
and says to them, "Let's celebrate! I've found
my lost sheep!" I can guarantee that there
will be more happiness in heaven over one
person who turns to God and changes the
way he thinks and acts than over 99 people
who already have turned to God
and have his approval.

LUKE 15:6-7 GOD'S WORD

Just As You
Are, My Child!

45

My Love for You

I love you without condition.

Beloved Daughter,

My love for you began even before you were born. From the moment I formed you in your mother's womb, and through every scraped knee and childhood joy, I was there, loving you and delighting in you. I was there as you grew into womanhood.

My heart broke when those who should have loved you did not. I wept when others who should have cared rejected you. But I was there, beloved, holding you, even when you did not know it. My love is perfect and unending. I will love you forever.

Faithfully yours,

Your Heavenly Father

You are precious in my sight,
and honored, and I love you,
I give people in return for you,
nations in exchange for your life.
ISAIAH 43:4 NRSV

*I trust your love, and I feel
like celebrating
because you rescued me.*
PSALM 13:5 CEV

The LORD appeared to me in a faraway place
and said, "I love you with an everlasting love.
So I will continue to show you my kindness."
JEREMIAH 31:3 GOD'S WORD

They *are* Your people and Your inheritance,
whom You brought out by Your mighty
power and by Your outstretched arm.
DEUTERONOMY 9:29 NKJV

Let your unfailing love comfort me,
just as you promised me, your servant.
PSALM 119:76 NLT

Your beauty and love chase after me
every day of my life.
I'm back home in the house of GOD
for the rest of my life.
PSALM 23:6 THE MESSAGE

God's Love

God's Love

I will sing of the LORD's great love forever;
with my mouth I will make your faithfulness
known through all generations.
I will declare that your love stands firm forever,
that you established your faithfulness in
heaven itself.

PSALM 89:1-2 NIV

Your love is faithful, LORD,
and even the clouds in the sky can
depend on you. . . .
Your love is a treasure, and everyone finds shelter
in the shadow of your wings.

PSALM 36:5,7 CEV

Great is your love, reaching to the heavens;
your faithfulness reaches to the skies.

PSALM 57:10 NIV

Satisfy us in the morning with your unfailing love,
so we may sing for joy to the end of our lives.

PSALM 90:14 NLT

As the Father has loved me, so I have loved you;
abide in my love.

JOHN 15:9 NRSV

I will maintain my love to him forever, and my
covenant with him will never fail.

PSALM 89:28 NIV

As for me, I shall sing of Your strength;
Yes, I shall joyfully sing of Your
lovingkindness in the morning,
For You have been my stronghold
And a refuge in the day of my distress.

PSALM 59:16 NASB

May you experience the love of Christ,
though it is so great you will never fully
understand it. Then you will be filled with
the fullness of life and power
that comes from God.

EPHESIANS 3:19 NLT

Cause me to hear thy lovingkindness in the
morning; for in thee do I trust; cause me to
know the way therein I should walk: for I lift
up my soul unto thee.

PSALM 143:8

How great is God's love for all who worship
him? Greater than the distance between
heaven and earth!

PSALM 103:11 CEV

My Love
for You

YOUR HANDS ARE MY HANDS

I do My work through you.

My Own,

I see how much you want to help others, but I also see your frustration as you wonder how one person can make a difference. You can because you are My daughter.

I do not call you to be successful. I call you only to be obedient, to touch one person at a time and to touch one family at a time, with My tangible love. Pray for My lambs daily, and do what you can, no matter how small the effort might seem. Keep in mind that if you give so much as a cup of water in My name, it is as if you are giving it to Me.

With compassion,

Your Heavenly Father

Work with enthusiasm, as though you were working for the Lord rather than for people.
EPHESIANS 6:7 NLT

Do not forget to do good and to share, for with such sacrifices God is well pleased.
HEBREWS 13:16 NKJV

Whoever speaks must speak God's words. Whoever serves must serve with the strength God supplies so that in every way God receives glory through Jesus Christ. Glory and power belong to Jesus Christ forever and ever!
1 PETER 4:11 GOD'S WORD

As for those who serve the Lord, he will redeem them; everyone who takes refuge in him will be freely pardoned.
PSALM 34:22 TLB

Share your food with everyone who is hungry; share your home with the poor and homeless. Give clothes to those in need; don't turn away your relatives.
ISAIAH 58:7 CEV

He comforts us in all our troubles so that we can comfort others. When others are troubled, we will be able to give them the same comfort God has given us.
2 CORINTHIANS 1:4 NLT

Helping Others

SEEK ME FIRST

I know what is best for you.

Dear One,

I gave you a wonderful capacity for decision-making. I gave you discernment, wisdom, and a heart that seeks a future filled with hope. Yet I have limited your human vision and knowledge. You cannot see what lies ahead.

This is where I come in, beloved. Seek Me first in all circumstances, in all relationships, and in every detail of your life. I know your past, your present, and your future. I know your heart intimately, and I know what is best. I will illuminate your path one step at a time, and I will lead you to blessings greater than you can imagine.

In all wisdom,

The Alpha and the Omega

Lead me in thy truth, and teach me: for thou
art the God of my salvation;
on thee do I wait all the day.
PSALM 25:5

With Your counsel
You will guide me,
And afterward receive
me to glory.
PSALM 73:24 NASB

You, LORD God, are my mighty rock
and my fortress.
Lead me and guide me,
so that your name will be honored.
Protect me from hidden traps
and keep me safe.
You are faithful,
and I trust you because you rescued me.
PSALM 31:3-5 CEV

What a blessing was that stillness
as he brought them safely into harbor!
Let them praise the LORD for his great love
and for all his wonderful deeds to them.
PSALM 107:30-31 NLT

I have taught you the way of wisdom.
I have guided you along decent paths.
When you walk, your stride
will not be hampered.
Even if you run, you will not stumble.
PROVERBS 4:11-12 GOD'S WORD

Guidance

Guidance

They shall not hunger nor thirst; neither shall the heat nor sun smite them: for he that hath mercy on them shall lead them, even by the springs of water shall he guide them.
ISAIAH 49:10

He is our God forever and ever,
and he will be our guide until we die.
PSALM 48:14 NLT

He guides the humble in what is right
and teaches them his way.
PSALM 25:9 NIV

Howbeit when he, the Spirit of truth, is come, he will guide you into all truth: for he shall not speak of himself; but whatsoever he shall hear, *that* shall he speak: and he will shew you things to come.
JOHN 16:13

Teach me to do your will, because you are my God.
May your good Spirit lead me on level ground.
PSALM 143:10 GOD'S WORD

God's love and kindness will shine upon us
like the sun that rises in the sky.
On us who live in the dark shadow of death
this light will shine
to guide us into a life of peace.
LUKE 1:78-79 CEV

From the ends of the earth I call to you,
I call as my heart grows faint;
lead me to the rock that is higher than I.
PSALM 61:2 NIV

I have seen their ways, but I will heal them;
I will lead them and repay them with comfort,
creating for their mourners the
fruit of the lips.
ISAIAH 57:18 NRSV

If I climb upward on the
rays of the morning sun
[or] land on the most distant shore of the sea
where the sun sets, even there your hand
would guide me
and your right hand would hold on to me.
PSALM 139:9-10 GOD'S WORD

If you obey my commands, you will remain in
my love, just as I have obeyed my Father's
commands and remain in his love.
JOHN 15:10 NIV

In all thy ways acknowledge
him, and he shall
direct thy paths.
PROVERBS 3:6

Seek Me First

A Lesson in Gardening

I will give you what you need.

Dear One,

You have poured out your heart to Me, for those you love, and for your own needs. You long to see visible and tangible answers to your heartfelt prayers. When you do not see change, you wonder if I am at work. Sometimes you doubt My care.

I have such a glorious lesson to teach you. Just as a seed planted in autumn is thought to be "dead" throughout the cold winter until the coming of spring and the bursting forth of new life, so it is sometimes with the hidden work I do. In My good time your answers will come, joyfully and miraculously. Be patient, dear one. I am at work even now.

Faithfully yours,

The Lord God

> I wait for the LORD, my soul does wait,
> And in His word do I hope.
> PSALM 130:5 NASB

In the morning, O LORD, you hear my voice; in the morning I lay my requests before you and wait in expectation.

PSALM 5:3 NIV

Righteous people flourish like palm trees and grow tall like the cedars in Lebanon. They are planted in the LORD'S house. They blossom in our God's courtyards. Even when they are old, they still bear fruit. They are always healthy and fresh.

PSALM 92:12-14 GOD'S WORD

He made a promise in the name of God who lives forever and who created heaven, earth, the sea, and every living creature. The angel said, "You won't have to wait any longer."

REVELATION 10:6 CEV

I waited and waited and waited for GOD.
At last he looked; finally he listened.
He lifted me out of the ditch,
pulled me from deep mud.
He stood me up on a solid rock
to make sure I wouldn't slip.

PSALM 40:1-2 THE MESSAGE

Patience

Patience

Be completely humble and gentle; be patient,
bearing with one another in love.
EPHESIANS 4:2 NIV

Even though the fig trees are all destroyed, and
there is neither blossom left nor fruit, and though
the olive crops all fail, and the fields lie barren; even
if the flocks die in the fields and the cattle barns are
empty, yet I will rejoice in the Lord; I will be happy
in the God of my salvation.
HABAKKUK 3:17-18 TLB

Break new ground.
Plant righteousness,
and harvest the fruit that your loyalty
will produce for me.
HOSEA 10:12 GOD'S WORD

It is not yet time for the message to come true,
but that time is coming soon;
the message will come true.
It may seem like a long time,
but be patient and wait for it,
because it will surely come;
it will not be delayed.
HABAKKUK 2:3 NCV

Finishing is better than starting!
Patience is better than pride!
ECCLESIASTES 7:8 TLB

You must be patient as you wait for the Lord's return. Consider the farmers who eagerly look for the rains in the fall and in the spring. They patiently wait for the precious harvest to ripen. You, too, must be patient. And take courage, for the coming of the Lord is near.

JAMES 5:7-8 NLT

He will give *you* rain for the seed which you will sow in the ground, and bread *from* the yield of the ground, and it will be rich and plenteous; on that day your livestock will graze in a roomy pasture.

ISAIAH 30:23 NASB

The rain cometh down, and the snow from heaven, and returneth not thither, but watereth the earth, and maketh it bring forth and bud, that it may give seed to the sower, and bread to the eater.

ISAIAH 55:10

Now may the Lord direct your hearts into the love of God and into the patience of Christ.

2 THESSALONIANS 3:5 NKJV

A Lesson in Gardening

AN INSTRUMENT OF MY PEACE

I bring peace to My children.

Beloved Daughter,

I long for all My children to know a full measure of My peace, but conflict and strife too often rule. I want to show them the difference that a real and lasting peace can bring into their lives.

It is through you, My child, that others can see Me. Just as a ripple expands in a pond, so will the influence of My peace—through you—touch the lives of others.

Today, consciously bring calming words to one troubled heart. Do the same tomorrow, and the day after tomorrow. Become My peacemaker, beloved, and watch My peace abound.

Shalom,

The God of Peace

> God blesses those who work for peace,
> for they will be called the children of God.
> MATTHEW 5:9 NLT

Let us pursue the things which make for peace and the building up of one another.
ROMANS 14:19 NASB

They will be so kind and merciful and good,
that they will be a light in the dark
for others who do the right thing.
PSALM 112:4 CEV

All this is from God. Through Christ, God
made peace between us and himself, and God
gave us the work of telling everyone about
the peace we can have with him.
2 CORINTHIANS 5:18 NCV

Wear shoes that are able to speed you on as
you preach the Good News of
peace with God.
EPHESIANS 6:15 TLB

Do not judge, and you will not be judged. Do
not condemn, and you will not be
condemned. Forgive, and you will be forgiven.
LUKE 6:37 NIV

Peacemaker

Peacemaker

In the same way let your light shine in front of people. Then they will see the good that you do and praise your Father in heaven.
MATTHEW 5:16 GOD'S WORD

The greatest among you shall be your servant. Whoever exalts himself shall be humbled; and whoever humbles himself shall be exalted.
MATTHEW 23:11-12 NASB

It is important to love him with all my heart and all my understanding and all my strength, and to love my neighbors as myself. This is more important than to offer all of the burnt offerings and sacrifices required in the law.
MARK 12:33 NLT

If you forgive others their trespasses, your heavenly Father will also forgive you.
MATTHEW 6:14 NRSV

Try to show as much compassion as your Father does.
LUKE 6:36 TLB

The fruit of the Spirit is love, joy, peace, patience, kindness, goodness, faithfulness, gentleness and self-control. Against such things there is no law.
GALATIANS 5:22-23 NIV

If your gift is that of serving others, serve them well. If you are a teacher, do a good job of teaching. If your gift is to encourage others, do it! If you have money, share it generously. If God has given you leadership ability, take the responsibility seriously. And if you have a gift for showing kindness to others, do it gladly.

ROMANS 12:7-8 NLT

Give, and you will receive. A large quantity, pressed together, shaken down, and running over will be put into your pocket. The standards you use for others will be applied to you.

LUKE 6:38 GOD'S WORD

When GOD approves of your life, even your enemies will end up shaking your hand.

PROVERBS 16:7 THE MESSAGE

Do not quarrel with anyone without cause, when no harm has been done to you.

PROVERBS 3:30 NRSV

An Instrument
of My Peace

LIFTED BY MY ANGELS

The nearness of My angels blesses you.

My Cherished One,

Consider My angels, those mighty and magnificent beings who were with Me at Creation, singing and joyfully shouting with the morning stars as I breathed life into the new earth. Today My angels live in My presence and do My bidding with never-ceasing joy and love for all of creation — including for you, too, My daughter.

Think of it, beloved! I planned from time's beginning for you to be blessed by the nearness of My angels! Think of My angels often, because they are My gift to you, to protect you and to lead you safely along your path.

With love,

The Lord Your God

He will send forth his angels with the sound of a mighty trumpet blast, and they will gather together his chosen ones from the farthest ends of the earth and heaven.

MATTHEW 24:31 NLT

*With all my heart I
praise you, LORD.
In the presence of angels
I sing your praises.*
PSALM 138:1 CEV

He dreamed that there was a ladder set up on
the earth, the top of it reaching to heaven; and
the angels of God were ascending and
descending on it. And the LORD stood beside
him and said, "I am the LORD, the God of
Abraham your father and the God of Isaac."
GENESIS 28:12-13 NRSV

Where were you when I made the
earth's foundation?
Tell me, if you understand.
Who marked off how big it should be?
Surely you know!
Who stretched a ruler across it?
What were the earth's foundations set on,
or who put its cornerstone in place
while the morning stars sang together
and all the angels shouted with joy?
JOB 38:4-7 NCV

He orders his angels to protect you
wherever you go.
PSALM 91:11 NLT

Angels

MY PURPOSE FOR YOU

I will show you My direction.

My Daughter,

Did you know that you are part of a plan, a plan set in motion before the beginning of time? All of creation is part of it.

Your place in this world is unique. I have created you to touch lives that no one else can touch. You can bring My grace, My forgiveness, My light, and My joy to those whose paths you cross.

That is not all. Magnificent riches are in store for you from now through eternity. Hold dear this thought: I have only begun to reveal My plan and purpose for you.

In infinite wisdom,

The Lord Your God

Eye hath not seen, nor ear heard, neither have entered into the heart of man, the things which God hath prepared for them that love him.

1 CORINTHIANS 2:9

You, LORD, are my God!
I will praise you for doing the
wonderful things
you had planned and promised
since ancient times.
ISAIAH 25:1 CEV

The counsel of the LORD stands forever,
the thoughts of his heart to all generations.
PSALM 33:11 NRSV

Do not conform any longer to the pattern of
this world, but be transformed by the renewing
of your mind. Then you will be able to test and
approve what God's will is—his good, pleasing
and perfect will.
ROMANS 12:2 NIV

The LORD All-Powerful has made this promise:
"These things will happen exactly as
I planned them;
they will happen exactly as I set them up."
ISAIAH 14:24 NCV

God saved us and called us to be holy, not
because of what we had done, but because of
his own plan and kindness.
2 TIMOTHY 1:9 GOD'S WORD

God's Plan

God's Plan

Who has performed and accomplished it,
Calling forth the generations from the beginning?
"I, the Lord, am the first,
and with the last. I am He."
ISAIAH 41:4 NASB

This truth gives them the confidence of eternal life,
which God promised them before the world
began—and he cannot lie.
TITUS 1:2 NLT

I am God! I can be trusted.
Your past troubles are gone;
I no longer think of them.
When you pray for someone to receive a blessing,
or when you make a promise,
you must do it in my name.
I alone am the God who can be trusted.
ISAIAH 65:16 CEV

Surely I know the plans I have for you, says the
LORD, plans for your welfare and not for harm, to
give you a future with hope. Then when you call
upon me and come and pray to me, I will hear you.
When you search for me, you will find me; if you
seek me with all your heart.
JEREMIAH 29:11-13 NRSV

"As the new heavens and the new earth
Which I will make shall remain
before Me," says the LORD,
"So shall your descendants and
your name remain."

ISAIAH 66:22 NKJV

Look at the birds of the air, that they do not
sow, neither do they reap, nor gather into
barns, and *yet* your heavenly Father feeds them.
Are you not worth much more than they?

MATTHEW 6:26 NASB

All this is proceeding along lines planned all
along by God and then executed in
Christ Jesus.

EPHESIANS 3:11 THE MESSAGE

We can make our plans, but the LORD
determines our steps.

PROVERBS 16:9 NLT

Christ brings a new agreement from God to his
people. Those who are called by God can now
receive the blessings he has
promised, blessings that will
last forever.

HEBREWS 9:15 NCV

My Purpose
for You

I Am Worthy of Your Adoration

Worship only Me.

Beloved Daughter,

I created you with a wondrous capacity to lift your heart in praise to your Creator. I long to bless you as you learn to praise Me.

When your thoughts turn to Me, other objects and desires that vie for your attention fade away. Your thoughts are given wing as you praise the only One worthy of your adoration.

I desire that you make praise a habit, yes, even a necessity. Through your heart-response to who I am, you will discover a wellspring of riches to fill your thirsty soul to overflowing.

Waiting by the waters,

The One Who Is Worthy of Praise

Oh, the joy of drinking deeply from the Fountain of Salvation! In that wonderful day you will say, "Thank the Lord! Praise his name! Tell the world about his wondrous love. How mighty he is!"

ISAIAH 12:3-4 TLB

I will praise the LORD
at all times.
I will constantly
speak his praises.
PSALM 34:1 NLT

Come, let's sing joyfully to the LORD.
Let's shout happily to the rock of our salvation.
Let's come into his presence with a song of
thanksgiving.
Let's shout happily to him with psalms.
PSALM 95:1-2 GOD'S WORD

Blessed be the LORD God, the God of Israel,
Who alone works wonders.
And blessed be His glorious name forever;
And may the whole earth be filled with His glory.
PSALM 72:18-19 NASB

God, we come into your Temple
to think about your love.
God, your name is known everywhere;
all over the earth people praise you.
Your right hand is full of goodness.
PSALM 48:9-10 NCV

We adore you as the one who is
over all things.
1 CHRONICLES 29:11 NLT

Worship

A Woman's Heart, Soul, and Mind

Love Me completely.

Dear One,

I have spoken of My deep love for you—its depth and breadth, how it existed before the beginning of time, and how it will continue throughout all eternity. What about your love for Me, beloved?

I desire that you love Me with your entire being. Love Me from that quiet place in your heart where your spirit dwells and where your emotions burst forth with laughter and song and feelings too deep to utter. Love Me with every breath you take and with every ounce of strength in your being.

Because of your deep love, you will know My voice and understand the words of love I whisper to your heart. You will be blessed beyond all measure!

In perfect love,

The Almighty

> My child, give me your heart,
> and let your eyes observe my ways.
> PROVERBS 23:26 NRSV

*I will be very kind for a
thousand lifetimes to those
who love me and
obey my commands.*
DEUTERONOMY 5:10 NCV

Love the LORD your God with all your heart,
with all your soul, and with all your strength.
Take to heart these words that I give you
today. Repeat them to your children. Talk
about them when you're at home or away,
when you lie down or get up.
DEUTERONOMY 6:5-7 GOD'S WORD

Let all who run to you for protection always
sing joyful songs. Provide shelter for those
who truly love you and let them rejoice.
PSALM 5:11 CEV

Know therefore that the LORD thy God, he *is*
God, the faithful God, which keepeth
covenant and mercy with them that love him
and keep his commandments
to a thousand generations.
DEUTERONOMY 7:9

LORD, HOW I love you! For you have done
such tremendous things for me.
PSALM 18:1 TLB

Loving God

Loving God

*I love all who love me. Those who search for me
will surely find me.*
PROVERBS 8:17 NLT

The LORD your God will cleanse your heart and the
hearts of all your descendants so that you will love
him with all your heart and soul,
and so you may live!
DEUTERONOMY 30:6 NLT

If you carefully obey the commands I am giving you
today and love the LORD your God and serve him
with your whole being, then he will send rain on
your land at the right time, in the fall and spring, and
you will be able to gather your grain, new wine, and
oil. He will put grass in the fields for your cattle,
and you will have plenty to eat.
DEUTERONOMY 11:13-15 NCV

Delight yourself in the LORD;
And He will give you the desires of your heart.
PSALM 37:4 NASB

Those who love me, I will deliver;
I will protect those who know my name.
PSALM 91:14 NRSV

I love the LORD, because he hath heard my voice
and my supplications.
PSALM 116:1

Choose to love the Lord your God and to obey
him and to cling to him, for he is your life and
the length of your days. You will then be able
to live safely in the land the Lord promised
your ancestors, Abraham, Isaac, and Jacob.

DEUTERONOMY 30:20 TLB

This is love: that we walk in obedience to his
commands. As you have heard from the
beginning, his command is that you walk in love.

2 JOHN 16 NIV

We know how much God loves us because we
have felt his love and because we believe him
when he tells us that he loves us dearly. God is
love, and anyone who lives in love is living with
God and God is living in him.

1 JOHN 4:16 TLB

Now, Israel, this is what the LORD your God
wants you to do: Respect the LORD your God,
and do what he has told you to do. Love him.
Serve the LORD your God
with your whole being.

DEUTERONOMY 10:12 NCV

A Woman's
Heart, Soul,
and Mind

SOUL-DEEP CONTENTMENT

My riches will give you joy.

Dearest Daughter,

I know you have a heart of gratitude. I smile when I hear your prayers of thanksgiving. In your gratitude for life's bigger blessings, however, do not overlook those simple pleasures that are also My gifts.

Raise your eyes to the setting sun and consider its glorious palette. Know that I created such color with you in mind. Gaze up at the canopy of stars and consider how they shone with Me at creation. Breathe in the fragrance of blooming lilacs and laugh with glorious delight that I knew even before your birth that you would take joy in their scent. Enjoy all My gifts, and your contentment will be soul-deep and lasting.

With love,

The Giver of Gifts

A godly life brings huge profits to people who are content with what they have. We didn't bring anything into the world, and we can't take anything out of it. As long as we have food and clothes, we should be satisfied.

I TIMOTHY 6:6-8 GOD'S WORD

*I said to the LORD, "You are
my Lord; apart from you I
have no good thing."*
PSALM 16:2 NIV

Go thy way, eat thy bread with joy, and drink thy
wine with a merry heart; for God now accepteth
thy works. Let thy garments be always white; and
let thy head lack no ointment. Live joyfully with
the wife whom thou lovest all the days of the life
of thy vanity, which he hath given thee under the
sun, all the days of thy vanity: for that *is* thy
portion in *this* life, and in thy labour which thou
takest under the sun.

ECCLESIASTES 9:7-9

I am not complaining about having too little. I
have learned to be satisfied with whatever I have.
I know what it is to be poor or to have plenty,
and I have lived under all kinds of conditions. I
know what it means to be full or to be hungry,
to have too much or too little.

PHILIPPIANS 4:11-12 CEV

LORD, you alone are my inheritance,
my cup of blessing.
You guard all that is mine.

PSALM 16:5 NLT

Contentment

Bring Me Your Every Need

Trust Me to help you.

My Own,

You struggle to bring your needs to Me.
Though you have trusted Me with your
heart, you are sometimes afraid of turning
over to Me other areas of your life, areas
such as broken relationships, family
concerns, or dying hopes and dreams.
Sometimes you hold on to your failures too,
afraid that if I pick you up, you might just
stumble again.

I am here to help you. There is no burden
too big for Me to carry, no heartache too
deep for My balm. If you stumble — and you
surely will — I am here for you to lean on.
Pour out your cares, and trust Me to help
you.

Worthy of your trust,

The Lord Your God

> Heed the sound of my cry for help,
> my King and my God,
> For to You I pray.
> PSALM 5:2 NASB

For you make me glad
by your deeds, O LORD;
I sing for joy at the
works of your hands.
PSALM 92:4 NIV

Our soul waits for the LORD;
He *is* our help and our shield.
For our heart shall rejoice in Him,
Because we have trusted in His holy name.
Let Your mercy, O LORD, be upon us,
Just as we hope in You.
PSALM 33:20-22 NKJV

You, in Your great compassion,
Did not forsake them in the wilderness;
The pillar of cloud did not leave them by day,
To guide them on their way,
Nor the pillar of fire by night, to light for
them the way in which they were to go.
You gave Your good Spirit to instruct them,
Your manna You did not withhold
from their mouth,
And You gave them water for their thirst.
NEHEMIAH 9:19-20 NASB

Thanks be to the Lord,
who daily carries our burdens for us.
God is our salvation.
PSALM 68:19 GOD'S WORD

God's Help

God's Help

He found them in a desert,
a windy, empty land.
He surrounded them and brought them up,
guarding them as those he loved very much.
He was like an eagle building its nest
that flutters over its young.
It spreads its wings to catch them
and carries them on its feathers.
DEUTERONOMY 32:10-11 NCV

The LORD, your Redeemer, the Holy One of Israel,
says: I am the LORD your God, who teaches you
what is good and leads you along the paths you
should follow.
ISAIAH 48:17 NLT

There is a river, the streams whereof shall make
glad the city of God, the holy *place* of the
tabernacles of the most High. God *is* in the midst of
her; she shall not be moved: God shall help her,
and that right early.
PSALM 46:4-5

You, O LORD, *are* a shield for me,
My glory and the One who lifts up my head.
PSALM 3:3 NKJV

God is my strong fortress;
And He sets the blameless in His way.
He makes my feet like hinds' *feet,*
And sets me on my high places.

2 SAMUEL 22:33-34 NASB

We thank you, God, we thank you—
your Name is our favorite word;
your mighty works are all we talk about.

PSALM 75:1 THE MESSAGE

O Lord my God, many and many a time you
have done great miracles for us, and we are
ever in your thoughts. Who else can do
such glorious things? No one else can be
compared with you. There isn't time to tell
of all your wonderful deeds.

PSALM 40:5 TLB

This God—his way is perfect;
the promise of the LORD proves true;
he is a shield for all who take refuge in him.

2 SAMUEL 22:31 NRSV

Bring Me Your
Every Need

I Wait for You

Give me your time, and I will transform you.

My Cherished One,

When we spend time alone, you receive riches. I delight when you set aside time during your busy day just to be with Me. When you seek Me alone in the late night or in the pale dawn, no distractions press in on you. I have your full attention, and you can learn of Me.

Come to Me with the quiet expectation of knowing Me better, and real change can begin — real change in your heart and life. You will be built up because of My strength, you will be filled with joy because of My joy, and your whole countenance will shine because you have seen My face.

Waiting for you,

Your Heavenly Father

My heart has heard you say,
"Come and talk with me."
And my heart responds, "LORD, I am coming."
PSALM 27:8 NLT

All that the Father giveth me
shall come to me; and him
that cometh to me I will in
no wise cast out.
JOHN 6:37

I've worked up such hunger and thirst for God,
traveling across dry and weary deserts.
So here I am in the place of worship,
eyes open, drinking in your strength and glory.
In your generous love I am really living at last!
My lips brim praises like fountains.
I bless you every time I take a breath;
My arms wave like banners of praise to you.
PSALM 63:2-3 THE MESSAGE

Let all who seek you
rejoice and be glad in you.
Let those who love your salvation
say evermore, "God is great!"
PSALM 70:4 NRSV

Happy are the people you choose
and invite to stay in your court.
We are filled with good things in your house,
your holy Temple.
PSALM 65:4 NCV

Seeking God

Seeking God

On God my salvation and my glory rest;
The rock of my strength, my refuge is in God.
Trust in Him at all times, O people;
Pour out your heart before Him;
God is a refuge for us.
PSALM 62:7-8 NASB

Let all who seek you rejoice and be glad
because of you.
Let those who love your salvation
continually say, "The LORD is great!"
PSALM 40:16 GOD'S WORD

Ask, and you will be given what you ask for. Seek,
and you will find. Knock, and the door will be
opened. For everyone who asks, receives. Anyone
who seeks, finds. If only you will knock, the door
will open.
MATTHEW 7:7-8 TLB

Likewise the Spirit helps us in our weakness; for we
do not know how to pray as we ought, but that
very Spirit intercedes with
sighs too deep for words.
ROMANS 8:26 NRSV

Seek the LORD while he may be found;
call on him while he is near.
ISAIAH 55:6 NIV

The LORD longs to be gracious to you;
he rises to show you compassion.
For the LORD is a God of justice.
Blessed are all who wait for him!

ISAIAH 30:18 NIV

Be glad that you are his;
let those who seek the LORD be happy.
Depend on the LORD and his strength;
always go to him for help.
Remember the miracles he has done;
remember his wonders and his decisions.

PSALM 105:3-5 NCV

Come to me with your ears wide open.
Listen, for the life of your soul is at stake. I
am ready to make an everlasting covenant
with you. I will give you all the mercies and
unfailing love that I promised to David.

ISAIAH 55:3 NLT

When you pray, go to your room and close
the door. Pray privately to your Father who
is with you. Your Father sees what you do in
private. He will reward you.

MATTHEW 6:6 GOD'S WORD

I Wait for You

SEASONS OF A WOMAN'S LIFE

I treasure you every day.

My Precious One,

Consider the seasons. Winter, with its new-fallen snow, covers the seeds of new life in its frozen depths. Spring, with its blossoms and trees, soon turns into summer's warm, long days. Then, before winter sets in again, autumn arrives with its dazzling show of color.

The rhythm of your life is like that, beloved. Your beauty in Me, your acts of love for others, your servant's heart, and your sacrifice of prayer will grow and change with each season of your life. There is glorious expectancy in such a plan. No season is more beautiful than another, but each is part of the life cycle I designed.

With you in your tomorrows,

The Lord God

> The steadfast love of the LORD never ceases,
> his mercies never come to an end;
> they are new every morning;
> great is your faithfulness.
> LAMENTATIONS 3:22-23 NRSV

God makes everything happen at
the right time. Yet none of us
can ever fully understand all
He has done, and He puts
questions in our minds about
the past and the future. I
know the best thing we can do is
to always enjoy life, because God's
gift to us is the happiness we get from our food
and drink and from the work we do.

ECCLESIASTES 3:11-13 CEV

There is a time for everything,
a season for every activity under heaven.
A time to be born and a time to die.
A time to plant and a time to harvest.
A time to kill and a time to heal.
A time to tear down and a time to rebuild.
A time to cry and a time to laugh.
A time to grieve and a time to dance.
A time to scatter stones
and a time to gather stones.
A time to embrace and a time to turn away.
A time to search and a time to lose.
A time to keep and a time to throw away.
A time to tear and a time to mend.
A time to be quiet and a time to speak up.
A time to love and a time to hate.
A time for war and a time for peace.

ECCLESIASTES 3:1-8 NLT

Expectancy

WHEN A FRIEND IS HURTING

My love can touch hearts.

My Own,

You are beginning to comprehend the depths of My love for you, a love that has to do with acts of compassion. But I want you to understand that one of the best ways to love Me is to love those I have placed around you.

When a friend is hurting, you may find it easy to minister to her with sacrificial love. But what about ministering to one who has hurt or despised you? Is she worthy of your compassion? This is the very love I have called you to. Express your compassion a step at a time. But be prepared. Such love changes lives.

Partners in love,

Your Heavenly Father

> These things I have spoken to you, that My joy may remain in you, and *that* your joy may be full. This is My commandment, that you love one another as I have loved you. Greater love has no one than this, than to lay down one's life for his friends.
>
> JOHN 15:11-13 NKJV

If you really keep the royal law found in Scripture, "Love your neighbor as yourself," you are doing right.

JAMES 2:8 NIV

The King shall answer and say unto them, Verily I say unto you, Inasmuch as ye have done *it* unto one of the least of these my brethren, ye have done *it* unto me.

MATTHEW 25:40

We love because he first loved us.

1 JOHN 4:19 NRSV

Regarding life together and getting along with each other, you don't need me to tell you what to do. You're *God*-taught in these matters. Just love one another! You're already good at it; your friends all over the province of Macedonia are the evidence. Keep it up; get better and better at it.

1 THESSALONIANS 4:9-10 THE MESSAGE

You have heard people say, "Love your neighbors and hate your enemies." But I tell you to love your enemies and pray for anyone who mistreats you.

MATTHEW 5:43-44 CEV

Compassion

Compassion

Anyone who gives one of my most humble followers a cup of cool water, just because that person is my follower, will surely be rewarded.
MATTHEW 10:42 CEV

In everything do to others as you would have them do to you; for this is the law and the prophets.
MATTHEW 7:12 NRSV

Whoever forgives an offense seeks love,
but whoever keeps bringing up the issue separates the closest of friends.
PROVERBS 17:9 GOD'S WORD

Continue to love each other with true Christian love.
HEBREWS 13:1 NLT

The one who blesses others is abundantly blessed; those who help others are helped.
PROVERBS 11:25 THE MESSAGE

Every one must make up his own mind as to how much he should give. Don't force anyone to give more than he really wants to, for cheerful givers are the ones God prizes.
2 CORINTHIANS 9:7 TLB

Dear children, we must show love through
actions that are sincere,
not through empty words.
1 JOHN 3:18 GOD'S WORD

I give you a new commandment, that you love
one another. Just as I have loved you, you
also should love one another. By this
everyone will know that you are my disciples,
if you have love for one another.
JOHN 13:34-35 NRSV

If you've gotten anything at all out of
following Christ, if his love has made any
difference in your life, if being in a community
of the Spirit means anything to you, if you
have a heart, if you *care*—then do me a favor:
Agree with each other, love each other, be
deep-spirited friends. Don't push your way to
the front; don't sweet-talk your way to the
top. Put yourself aside, and help others get
ahead. Don't be obsessed with getting your
own advantage. Forget yourselves long
enough to lend a helping hand.
PHILIPPIANS 2:1-4 THE MESSAGE

When a Friend
Is Hurting

COME AWAY

Draw near to Me.

My Treasure,

I am Almighty God, Creator of earth and everything on it. I flung the stars across the heavens and hung the sun and moon. I am also your Heavenly Father, your Papa, who knit you together in your mother's womb. I know you inside and out. I know your hopes, your dreams, and your triumphs. I know your heartaches, your sorrows, and your disappointments.

I long to draw you close and hold you in My lap, just as My Son once held the little children by Galilee. In My nearness you will find joy, comfort, and blessings beyond measure. You will find total acceptance, for I love you.

Joyfully,

The One Who Knows You

> I *am* my beloved's, and his desire is toward me.
> THE SONG OF SOLOMON 7:10

*I will also do this thing that
you have spoken; for you
have found grace in My sight,
and I know you by name.*
EXODUS 33:17 NKJV

You created my inmost being;
you knit me together in my mother's womb.
I praise you because I am fearfully and
wonderfully made;
your works are wonderful,
I know that full well.
PSALM 139:13-14 NIV

We are His workmanship, created in Christ
Jesus unto good works, which God hath before
ordained that we should walk in them.
EPHESIANS 2:10

Your eyes saw me when I was only a fetus.
Every day [of my life] was recorded
in your book
before one of them had taken place.
PSALM 139:16 GOD'S WORD

The Lord will work out his plans for my life—
for your lovingkindness, Lord, continues
forever. Don't abandon me—for you made me.
PSALM 138:8 TLB

Intimacy with God

Intimacy with God

You know me inside and out,
you know every bone in my body;
You know exactly how I was made, bit by bit,
how I was sculpted from nothing into something.
PSALM 139:15 THE MESSAGE

God created human beings in his image. In the
image of God he created them. He created them
male and female.
GENESIS 1:27 NCV

Just as you do not know how the breath comes to
the bones in the mother's womb, so you do not
know the work of God, who makes everything.
ECCLESIASTES 11:5 NRSV

I am the good shepherd. I know my sheep, as the
Father knows me. And my sheep know me, as I
know the Father. I give my life for the sheep.
JOHN 10:14-15 NCV

You, Lord, are good, and ready to forgive,
And abundant in lovingkindness
to all who call upon You.
Give ear, O LORD, to my prayer;
And give heed to the voice of my supplications!
In the day of my trouble I shall call upon You,
For You will answer me.
PSALM 86:5-7 NASB

Now we see but a poor reflection as in a
mirror; then we shall see face to face. Now I
know in part; then I shall know fully,
even as I am fully known.

1 CORINTHIANS 13:12 NIV

I knew you before I formed you in your
mother's womb. Before you were born I set
you apart and appointed you as my
spokesman to the world.

JEREMIAH 1:5 NLT

Little children were brought for Jesus to lay
his hands on them and pray. But the disciples
scolded those who brought them. "Don't
bother him," they said. But Jesus said, "Let the
little children come to me, and don't prevent
them. For of such is the Kingdom of Heaven."
And he put his hands on their heads and
blessed them before he left.

MATTHEW 19:13-15 TLB

You never saw him, yet you love him. You still
don't see him, yet you trust him—with
laughter and singing. Because you
kept on believing, you'll get
what you're looking forward
to: total salvation.

1 PETER 1:8 THE MESSAGE

Come Away

One Silent Night

Trust in My promises.

Dear One,

Mary once received astounding news from the angel Gabriel. Because she believed My promise, she had hope in her heart during her pregnancy, the mean circumstances of her Son's birth, and her Son's childhood. When her Son grew to adulthood, she endured the greatest sorrow a mother could know, and yet she never lost hope, even as her precious Child died.

The world around you is often one of turmoil and suffering, even tragedy. It is easy to doubt that I am still at work and that My promise to you will be carried out. But keep your eyes on Me, no matter what happens around you. Believe in My promises. They are as real today as they were to My daughter Mary.

With infinite love,

The One Mighty to Save

When Jesus saw his mother there, and the disciple whom he loved standing nearby, he said to his mother, "Dear woman, here is your son."

JOHN 19:26 NIV

*You are blessed for believing
that the Lord would keep
his promise to you.*
LUKE 1:45 GOD'S WORD

The angel said to her, "Do not be afraid, Mary;
for you have found favor with God. And behold,
you will conceive in your womb and bear a son,
and you shall name Him Jesus. He will be great
and will be called the Son of the Most High; and
the Lord God will give Him the throne of His
father David; and He will reign over the house of
Jacob forever, and His kingdom will have no end."
LUKE 1:30-33 NASB

So they hurried off and found Mary and Joseph,
and the baby, who was lying in the manger. When
they had seen him, they spread the word
concerning what had been told them about this
child, and all who heard it were amazed at what
the shepherds said to them. But Mary treasured
up all these things and pondered them in
her heart.
LUKE 2:16-19 NIV

Hope

I REJOICE OVER YOU WITH SINGING

You bring delight to My heart.

My Own,

You bring me joy, although you cannot earn this joy. You do not have to be perfect, and, indeed, no one can be. No, My precious one, My joy is complete simply because I love you and enjoy watching you learn of Me, grow in Me, and seek to do My will.

Joy is contagious. Because I have great joy, I fill your heart with songs of rejoicing. And because you love Me, My joy spills forth to others through little acts of kindness and mercy. It brings delight to Me to see you reflect My character. You gladden My heart. Even now, I am singing with joy over you.

Joyfully,

Your Heavenly Father

The LORD your God is with you,
he is mighty to save.
He will take great delight in you,
he will quiet you with his love,
he will rejoice over you with singing.
ZEPHANIAH 3:17 NIV

Through each day the LORD pours
his unfailing love upon me,
and through each night
I sing his songs,
praying to God
who gives me life.
PSALM 42:8 NLT

Because of what Christ has done we have
become gifts to God that he delights in, for as
part of God's sovereign plan we were chosen
from the beginning to be his, and all things
happen just as he decided long ago.
EPHESIANS 1:11 TLB

The ransomed of the LORD will return
And come with joyful shouting to Zion,
With everlasting joy upon their heads.
They will find gladness and joy,
And sorrow and sighing will flee away.
ISAIAH 35:10 NASB

O LORD, God of Israel, there is no God like you
in heaven or on earth—you who keep your
covenant of love with your servants who
continue wholeheartedly in your way.
2 CHRONICLES 6:14 NIV

God's Joy

TOUCH SOMEONE'S LIFE TODAY

With Me, you can make a difference.

Dear One,

I see your caring heart and know that you want to touch the lives of those around you. In today's hustle and bustle, however, people have little time to listen. You wonder how your life can make any difference when people appear to have little interest in Me and the riches I have for them.

I have a secret to share. Begin with something small—a smile or gracious word—and touch one heart at a time. Believe Me, even the smallest act given in love can turn into something big.

In love,

The Lord of All

When she speaks, her words are wise,
and kindness is the rule
when she gives instructions.
PROVERBS 31:26 NLT

*A kindhearted woman
gains respect,
but ruthless men gain
only wealth.*
PROVERBS 11:16 NIV

Be kind to one another, tender-hearted, forgiving
each other, just as God in Christ also has
forgiven you.
EPHESIANS 4:32 NASB

Love is very patient and kind, never jealous or
envious, never boastful or proud.
1 CORINTHIANS 13:4 TLB

When you're kind to others, you help yourself;
when you're cruel to others, you hurt yourself.
PROVERBS 11:17 THE MESSAGE

Being kind to the poor is like
lending to the LORD;
he will reward you for what you have done.
PROVERBS 19:17 NCV

The good person is generous and lends lavishly;
No shuffling or stumbling around for this one,
But a sterling and solid and lasting reputation.
PSALM 112:5-6 THE MESSAGE

Kindness

LEARN OF ME

My riches are yours.

Beloved Daughter,

Do you know that I love to reveal Myself to you? Look around, beloved, and know Me through what I do—from the beauty of My creation to the beauty in your soul. I delight in your knowledge of me. Study My Word, and discover My promises.

Through My Word you will uncover the mysteries of My character. Taste My glory, My wisdom, My power, My grace, My justice, My truth, My majesty, and My love. Learn of My Son, whom I sent so you could know Me. Learn of My Holy Spirit, who is with you even now. You will find great contentment, and you will find rest for your soul.

With power and might,

The One Who Never Changes

I desire mercy and not sacrifice,
And the knowledge of God more
than burnt offerings.
HOSEA 6:6 NKJV

The Lord is good to everyone.
He showers compassion on
all his creation.
PSALM 145:9 NLT

Be still, and know that I am God;
I will be exalted among the nations,
I will be exalted in the earth.
PSALM 46:10 NIV

Thus says the LORD: Do not let the wise boast
in their wisdom, do not let the mighty boast in
their might, do not let the wealthy boast in
their wealth; but let those who boast boast in
this, that they understand and know me, that I
am the LORD; I act with steadfast love, justice,
and righteousness in the earth, for in these
things I delight, says the LORD.
JEREMIAH 9:23-24 NRSV

I will give you the wealth that is stored away
and the hidden riches
so you will know I am the LORD,
the God of Israel, who calls you by name.
ISAIAH 45:3 NCV

Knowing God

Knowing God

*Pour out your unfailing love on those who know
you! Never stop giving your salvation to those
who long to do your will.*

PSALM 36:10 TLB

I will make rivers flow on barren heights,
and springs within the valleys.
I will turn the desert into pools of water,
and the parched ground into springs.

ISAIAH 41:18 NIV

All Your works shall give thanks to You, O LORD,
And Your godly ones shall bless You.
They shall speak of the glory of Your kingdom
And talk of Your power.

PSALM 145:10-11 NASB

The LORD is fair in all his ways
and faithful in everything he does.

PSALM 145:17 GOD'S WORD

My thoughts are not your thoughts,
nor are your ways my ways, says the LORD.
For as the heavens are higher than the earth,
so are my ways higher than your ways
and my thoughts than your thoughts.

ISAIAH 55:8-9 NRSV

Realize that the LORD alone is God.
He made us, and we are his.
We are his people and the sheep in his care.
PSALM 100:3 GOD'S WORD

You know about the kindness of our Lord
Jesus Christ. He was rich, yet for your sake
he became poor in order to make you rich
through his poverty.
2 CORINTHIANS 8:9 GOD'S WORD

The LORD is gracious and righteous;
our God is full of compassion.
PSALM 116:5 NIV

God's mercy is great, and he loved us very
much. Though we were spiritually dead
because of the things we did against God, he
gave us new life with Christ. You have been
saved by God's grace.
EPHESIANS 2:4-5 NCV

The lovingkindness of the Lord is from
everlasting to everlasting, to those who
reverence him; his salvation is to children's
children of those who are faithful
to his covenant and remember
to obey him!
PSALM 103:17-18 TLB

Learn of Me

YOUR TOMORROWS ARE IN MY HANDS

Trust Me with everything.

Dear One,

You wonder sometimes about your tomorrows. You have questions about the future of your family, your children, your husband, and your aging parents. Your loving heart is concerned about them.

My child, I have good news. I am in control. There is never a moment that you and the ones you love are not in the center of My thoughts. Trust Me to lead you and all those precious to you one day at a time. The future is not yours to know—and I have good reasons for that—but I assure you that a joyous journey lies ahead. Take My hand and walk with Me in utter and complete trust. Discover My will for you hour by hour.

Still leading,

He Who Loves You

> I depended on you before I was born.
> You took me from my mother's womb.
> My songs of praise constantly speak about you.
> PSALM 71:6 GOD'S WORD

Don't ever worry about tomorrow.
After all, tomorrow will worry
about itself. Each day has
enough trouble
of its own.
MATTHEW 6:34 GOD'S WORD

The eyes of all mankind look up to you for help;
you give them their food as they need it. You
constantly satisfy the hunger and thirst
of every living thing.
PSALM 145:15-16 TLB

Why do you worry about clothes? Look at how
the lilies in the field grow. They don't work or
make clothes for themselves. But I tell you that
even Solomon with his riches was not dressed as
beautifully as one of these flowers.
MATTHEW 6:28-29 NCV

Trust in the LORD and do good.
Then you will live safely in the land and prosper.
Take delight in the LORD,
and he will give you your heart's desires.
Commit everything you do to the LORD.
Trust him, and he will help you.
PSALM 37:3-5 NLT

God's Faithfulness

Joyful Adoration

I lighten your burdens and give you strength.

My Beloved,

Do you know why praising Me is important in your life? Let Me share a secret with you. It is not for Me that I require your praise. It is for you.

Praising Me moves your eyes from your present circumstances to the One who will help you. Focus on My glory, My strength, and My help in ages past. Know that Almighty God is with you today.

Joy is Mine as I see your countenance transformed from worry to one of utter peace. Your burdens become noticeably lighter as you sing of My mercies, and so praise Me often, daughter. Lift your voice in thanksgiving and song.

Most joyously,

The Exalted One

Praise the LORD!
How good it is to sing praises to our God!
How delightful and how right!
PSALM 147:1 NLT

I WILL PRAISE you, my God and King, and bless your name each day and forever.
PSALM 145:1-2 TLB

I will give thanks to the LORD with all my heart;
I will tell of all Your wonders.
I will be glad and exult in You;
I will sing praise to Your name, O Most High.
PSALM 9:1-2 NASB

Your great love reaches to the skies,
your truth to the heavens.
God, you are supreme above the skies.
Let your glory be over all the earth.
PSALM 108:4-5 NCV

Your awe-inspiring deeds
will be on every tongue;
I will proclaim your greatness.
Everyone will share the story of your
wonderful goodness;
they will sing with joy of your righteousness.
PSALM 145:6-7 NLT

God is alive! Praise him who is the
great rock of protection.
PSALM 18:46 TLB

Praising God

Praising God

It is good to praise you, Lord,
to sing praises to God Most High.
It is good to tell of your love in the morning
and of your loyalty at night.
It is good to praise you with the ten-stringed lyre
and with the soft-sounding harp.

PSALM 92:1-3 NCV

My heart is steadfast, O God;
I will sing and make music with all my soul.

PSALM 108:1 NIV

PRAISE THE LORD, all nations everywhere. Praise him,
all the peoples of the earth. For he loves us very
dearly, and his truth endures. Praise the Lord.

PSALM 117 TLB

I will praise you, LORD, for you have rescued me.
You refused to let my enemies triumph over me.
O LORD my God, I cried out to you for help,
and you restored my health.

PSALM 30:1-2 NLT

Awake, harp and lyre;
I will awaken the dawn!
I will give thanks to You, O LORD,
among the peoples,
And I will sing praises to You among the nations.

PSALM 108:2-3 NASB

O LORD OUR God, the majesty and glory of
your name fills all the earth and overflows
the heavens. You have taught the little
children to praise you perfectly. May their
example shame and silence your enemies!
PSALM 8:1-2 TLB

Shout praises to the LORD!
He is good to us, and his love never fails.
Everyone the LORD has rescued
from trouble
should praise him.
PSALM 107:1-2 CEV

My mouth will speak in praise of the LORD.
Let every creature praise his holy name
for ever and ever.
PSALM 145:21 NIV

Sing to the LORD, you who do what is right;
honest people should praise him.
Praise the LORD on the harp;
make music for him on a ten-stringed lyre.
Sing a new song to him;
play well and joyfully.
PSALM 33:1-3 NCV

Joyful Adoration

LET MY SPIRIT SHINE THROUGH YOU

I will perform mighty works within you.

My Own,

I have given you a precious gift. The Holy Spirit is your spirit's source of encouragement and power and strength. When you hear My voice, My Holy Spirit is whispering in your heart. Draw close to Me and learn.

As you invite Him to do so, beloved, My Holy Spirit will perform mighty works within you. Precious one, listen for My still, small voice; open your heart to My promptings; let Me strengthen and empower you. Others will see Me, and your countenance will utterly shine with My Spirit in you.

With power and might,

The Lord Your God

There are different kinds of spiritual gifts, but they all come from the same Spirit. There are different ways to serve the same Lord, and we can each do different things. Yet the same God works in all of us and helps us in everything we do. The Spirit has given each of us a special way of serving others.

1 CORINTHIANS 12:4-7 CEV

You are the world's light—a city on a hill, glowing in the night for all to see.
MATTHEW 5:14 TLB

If we are living in the light of God's presence, just as Christ is, then we have fellowship with each other, and the blood of Jesus, his Son, cleanses us from every sin.
1 JOHN 1:7 NLT

"Streams of living water will flow from deep within the person who believes in me." Jesus said this about the Spirit, whom his believers would receive. The Spirit was not yet evident, as it would be after Jesus had been glorified.
JOHN 7:38-39 GOD'S WORD

"As for me, this is my covenant with them," says the LORD. "My Spirit, who is on you, and my words that I have put in your mouth will not depart from your mouth, or from the mouths of your children, or from the mouths of their descendants from this time on and forever," says the LORD.
ISAIAH 59:21 NIV

Holy Spirit

A Forgiving Heart

Forgive as I forgive.

Beloved,

My forgiveness was given to you long ago. Just as I have forgiven you, I want you to extend the gift of forgiveness to others. Do this even before anyone asks for your forgiveness.

Believe Me when I tell you that it is important to forgive right away. If you hold on to your hurts and grudges, you will only experience deep grief, for an unforgiving heart can turn bitter. Do not let that happen to you. Let Me help you forgive quickly and quietly. Give your heartache to Me. I am here to help you. I am here to restore peace to your spirit.

With grace,

The One Who Gave His Son

Those with good sense are slow to anger,
and it is their glory to overlook an offense.
PROVERBS 19:11 NRSV

God is faithful and reliable.
If we confess our sins, he
forgives them and cleanses us
from everything we've
done wrong.
1 JOHN 1:9 GOD'S WORD

Whenever you stand praying, forgive, if you
have anything against anyone, so that your
Father who is in heaven will also forgive you
your transgressions.

MARK 11:25 NASB

Be gentle and ready to forgive; never hold
grudges. Remember, the Lord forgave you, so
you must forgive others.

COLOSSIANS 3:13 TLB

To whom ye forgive any thing, I *forgive* also:
for if I forgave any thing, to whom I forgave *it*,
for your sakes *forgave I it* in the
person of Christ.

2 CORINTHIANS 2:10

You have heard that it was said, "Love your
neighbor and hate your enemies." But I say to
you, love your enemies. Pray for those
who hurt you.

MATTHEW 5:43-44 NCV

Forgiveness

Forgiveness

*I say to you who hear: Love your enemies, do good
to those who hate you, bless those who curse you,
and pray for those who spitefully use you.*

LUKE 6:27-28 NKJV

Don't repay evil for evil. Don't retaliate when
people say unkind things about you. Instead, pay
them back with a blessing. That is what God wants
you to do, and he will bless you for it.

1 PETER 3:9 NLT

This is how you should pray:
Our Father in heaven,
let your name be kept holy.
Let your kingdom come.
Let your will be done on earth
as it is done in heaven.
Give us our daily bread today.
Forgive us as we forgive others.

MATTHEW 6:9-12 GOD'S WORD

Then said Jesus, Father, forgive them; for they know
not what they do. And they parted his raiment,
and cast lots.

LUKE 23:34

This is how my heavenly Father will treat each of
you unless you forgive your brother
from your heart.

MATTHEW 18:35 NIV

Peter came up to the Lord and asked, "How many times should I forgive someone who does something wrong to me? Is seven times enough?" Jesus answered: Not just seven times, but seventy-seven times.

MATTHEW 18:21-22 CEV

Whenever you stand praying, forgive, if you have anything against anyone; so that your Father in heaven may also forgive you your trespasses.

MARK 11:25 NRSV

Love your enemies and be good to them. Lend without expecting to be paid back. Then you will get a great reward, and you will be the true children of God in heaven. He is good even to people who are unthankful and cruel.

LUKE 6:35 CEV

If your enemy is hungry,
give him some food to eat,
and if he is thirsty,
give him some water to drink.
[In this way] you will make him feel
guilty and ashamed, and the LORD
will reward you.

PROVERBS 25:21-22
GOD'S WORD

A Forgiving
Heart

MY STRENGTH IN YOUR WEARINESS

I am sufficient.

My Own,

The roles in your life can sometimes threaten to overwhelm you. You try to fit more hours into your day just to meet the responsibilities that are most important to you—the responsibilities to your family, your home, your career, and your friendships.

My daughter, nothing is more important than your relationship with Me. I am sufficient to meet all your needs. When you come to Me first, I will give you the strength you need to deal with the demands on your time.

Let Me fill you with resources you can find nowhere else. The resources that you draw from Me will help you in every realm of your life and give you a deep spirit-rest.

More than enough,

The Great Provider

> *It is* God that girdeth me with strength, and maketh my way perfect. He maketh my feet like hinds' *feet*, and setteth me upon my high places.
>
> PSALM 18:32-33

All of you worship the Lord,
so you must trust him
to help and protect you.
PSALM 115:11 CEV

GOD is bedrock under my feet,
the castle in which I live,
my rescuing knight.
My God—the high crag
where I run for dear life,
hiding behind the boulders,
safe in the granite hideout.
I sing to GOD, the Praise-Lofty,
and find myself safe and saved.

PSALM 18:2-3 THE MESSAGE

I want you to know about the great and
mighty power that God has for us followers.
It is the same wonderful power he used when
he raised Christ from death and let him sit at
his right side in heaven. There Christ rules
over all forces, authorities, powers, and
rulers. He rules over all beings in this world
and will rule in the future world as well.

EPHESIANS 1:19-21 CEV

Sufficiency

Sufficiency

Blessed are you *who hunger now,*
For you shall be filled.
Blessed are you *who weep now,*
For you shall laugh.
LUKE 6:21 NKJV

Search for the LORD and for his strength,
and keep on searching.
PSALM 105:4 NLT

I was right on the cliff-edge, ready to fall,
when GOD grabbed and held me.
GOD's my strength, he's also my song,
and now he's my salvation.
PSALM 118:13-14 THE MESSAGE

You will give me added years of life, as rich and full
as those of many generations, all packed into one.
And I shall live before the Lord forever. Oh, send
your lovingkindness and truth to
guard and watch over me.
PSALM 61:6-7 TLB

I will give you the words I want you to say.
I will cover you with my hands and protect you.
I made the heavens and the earth,
and I say to Jerusalem, "You are my people."
ISAIAH 51:16 NCV

He fills my life with good things.
My youth is renewed like the eagle's!
PSALM 103:5 NLT

The LORD is my strength and my shield;
my heart trusts in him, and I am helped.
My heart leaps for joy
and I will give thanks to him in song.
The LORD is the strength of his people,
a fortress of salvation for his anointed one.
Save your people and bless your inheritance;
be their shepherd and carry them forever.
PSALM 28:7-9 NIV

I will reflect on all your actions
and think about what you have done. . . .
You are the God who performs miracles.
You have made your strength
known among the nations.
PSALM 77:12,14 GOD'S WORD

I can do everything with the help of Christ
who gives me the strength I need.
PHILIPPIANS 4:13 NLT

When I pray, you answer me;
you encourage me by giving
me the strength I need.
PSALM 138:3 NLT

My Strength in
Your Weariness

A HEART FILLED WITH GRACE

I am not finished with you.

My Cherished One,

Grace is a heart-acceptance that looks at others with the spirit of compassion. Grace is love given freely, without limit, without condition.

This is the foundation of My love for you, beloved. Because of My grace, you stand perfect and beautiful in My sight. But I am not finished with you. I will continue to work in your heart all your days on earth.

While I am working within you, extend grace to others. Know that I am not yet finished with them either. They will see My love shining through you. Your heart—and theirs—will be blessed as you understand the meaning of grace.

With all generosity,

The One Who Loves Completely

From the fullness of his grace we have all
received one blessing after another.

JOHN 1:16 NIV

His anger endureth *but a
moment; in his favour is life:
weeping may endure for a night,
but joy* cometh *in the morning.*
PSALM 30:5

Remember, O LORD, your unfailing
love and compassion,
which you have shown from long ages past.
Forgive the rebellious sins of my youth;
look instead through the
eyes of your unfailing love,
for you are merciful, O LORD.
PSALM 25:6-7 NLT

This righteousness from God comes through
faith in Jesus Christ to all who believe. There
is no difference, for all have sinned and fall
short of the glory of God, and are justified
freely by his grace through the redemption
that came by Christ Jesus.
ROMANS 3:22-24 NIV

Open your ears and listen, my God. Open
your eyes and look at our ruins and at the
city called by your name. We are not
requesting this from you because we are
righteous, but because you are
very compassionate.
DANIEL 9:18 GOD'S WORD

Grace

Grace

I give thanks to my God always for you because of the grace of God that has been given you in Christ Jesus, for in every way you have been enriched in him, in speech and knowledge of every kind.

1 CORINTHIANS 1:4-5 NRSV

May the Master pour on the love so it fills your lives and splashes over on everyone around you, just as it does from us to you.

1 THESSALONIANS 3:12 THE MESSAGE

God blesses those who are hungry and thirsty
for justice,
for they will receive it in full.
God blesses those who are merciful,
for they will be shown mercy.

MATTHEW 5:6-7 NLT

God raised us up with Christ and seated us with him in the heavenly realms in Christ Jesus, in order that in the coming ages he might show the incomparable riches of his grace, expressed in his kindness to us in Christ Jesus.

EPHESIANS 2:6-7 NIV

Grace and peace be multiplied unto you through the knowledge of God, and of Jesus our Lord.

2 PETER 1:2

He said unto me, My grace is sufficient for thee: for my strength is made perfect in weakness. Most gladly therefore will I rather glory in my infirmities, that the power of Christ may rest upon me.

2 CORINTHIANS 12:9

Blessed *are* the pure in heart:
for they shall see God.

MATTHEW 5:8

The sin of this one man, Adam, caused death to rule over us, but all who receive God's wonderful, gracious gift of righteousness will live in triumph over sin and death through this one man, Jesus Christ.

ROMANS 5:17 NLT

Blessed are those who recognize
they are spiritually helpless.
The kingdom of heaven belongs to them.
Blessed are those who mourn.
They will be comforted.
Blessed are those who are gentle.
They will inherit the earth.

MATTHEW 5:3-5
GOD'S WORD

A Heart Filled with Grace

YOUR BATTLES ARE MINE

Bring Me your every need.

My Child,

You long for strength to help you through your struggles. Some of those battles have to do with your inner self; some have to do with relationships and responsibilities; some have to do with financial struggles and career challenges.

Bring every struggle to Me, daughter. Talk to Me about each concern. I will help you identify those things that need changing in your life. I will help you be strong in those areas where you feel you are weak. Give all your battles to Me, and watch Me work on your behalf. Do not be afraid. I am with you.

In power and strength,

The Almighty

> You won't even have to fight. Just take your positions and watch the LORD rescue you from your enemy. Don't be afraid. Just do as you're told. And as you march out tomorrow, the Lord will be there with you.
>
> 2 CHRONICLES 20:17 CEV

My flesh and my heart fail;
But God is the strength of
my heart and my portion
forever.

PSALM 73:26 NKJV

The Lord is my strength, my song,
and my salvation.
He is my God, and I will praise him.
He is my father's God—I will exalt him.

EXODUS 15:2 TLB

May your hearts be made strong so that you will
be holy and without fault before our God and
Father when our Lord Jesus comes
with all his holy ones.

I THESSALONIANS 3:13 NCV

I STAND SILENTLY before the Lord, waiting for him
to rescue me. For salvation comes from him
alone. Yes, he alone is my Rock, my rescuer,
defense and fortress. Why then should I be tense
with fear when troubles come?

PSALM 62:1-2 TLB

God can guard you so that you don't fall and so
that you can be full of joy as you stand in his
glorious presence without fault.

JUDE 24 GOD'S WORD

Power

I cherish you.

My Treasured One,

I desire that you keep your eyes on Me, your Father-King, and know that you are made in My image. You are the daughter of Almighty God; you are a child of royal heritage. Imagine it, precious one. I sent My Son as a ransom for you. What greater value can there be? You are My cherished possession, and I long to shower you with gifts and good things that are available only to My children.

Let Me reveal your true beauty through your character. Let the traits of your heritage shine through. Let Me shine through you every day in kind deeds, humility, patience, and gentle words.

With all glory and honor,

Your Father-King

> You are a people holy to the LORD your God.
> Out of all the peoples on the face of the earth,
> the LORD has chosen you
> to be his treasured possession.
> DEUTERONOMY 14:2 NIV

Let the teaching of Christ live in you richly. Use all wisdom to teach and instruct each other by singing psalms, hymns, and spiritual songs with thankfulness in your hearts to God.

COLOSSIANS 3:16 NCV

We also have joy with our troubles, because we know that these troubles produce patience. And patience produces character, and character produces hope. And this hope will never disappoint us, because God has poured out his love to fill our hearts. He gave us his love through the Holy Spirit, whom God has given to us.

ROMANS 5:3-5 NCV

In everything you do, stay away from complaining and arguing, so that no one can speak a word of blame against you. You are to live clean, innocent lives as children of God in a dark world full of people who are crooked and stubborn. Shine out among them like beacon lights.

PHILIPPIANS 2:14-15 TLB

Let me rejoice in the joy of your people; let me praise you with those who are your heritage.

PSALM 106:5 NLT

Character

TAKE COURAGE

I will strengthen you.

My Beloved,

When you face trials, consider that you are in training. Stop for a moment, dear one, and think about your challenges from this different perspective: consider dealing with adversity as strength training for your spirit, in much the same way that lifting weights builds strong bones or jogging aerobically exercises the cardiovascular system.

A long-distance runner pushes her body beyond what she thinks she can endure. Yet when she reaches her goal, her months or years of training make her trials worthwhile. Rejoice and welcome the challenges ahead. Know that I am with you and will give you strength for each step of the way.

In love,

Your Personal Trainer

Be of good courage, and he shall strengthen your heart, all ye that hope in the Lord.
PSALM 31:24

Be on guard. Stand true to what you believe. Be courageous. Be strong. And everything you do must be done with love.
1 CORINTHIANS 16:13-14 NLT

Stand united, singular in vision, contending for people's trust in the Message, the good news, not flinching or dodging in the slightest before the opposition. Your courage and unity will show them what they're up against: defeat for them, victory for you—and both because of God.
PHILIPPIANS 1:27-28 THE MESSAGE

God did not give us a spirit of timidity, but a spirit of power, of love and of self-discipline.
2 TIMOTHY 1:7 NIV

In the fear of the LORD there is
strong confidence,
and his children will have a place of refuge.
PROVERBS 14:26 GOD'S WORD

I pray that, according to the riches of his glory, he may grant that you may be strengthened in your inner being with power through his Spirit.
EPHESIANS 3:16 NRSV

Courage

Courage

I called upon the Lord in distress: the Lord answered me, and set me in a large place. The Lord is on my side; I will not fear: what can man do unto me?

PSALM 118:5-6

Continue to live in fellowship with Christ so that when he returns, you will be full of courage and not shrink back from him in shame.

1 JOHN 2:28 NLT

You've all been to the stadium and seen the athletes race. Everyone runs; one wins. Run to win. All good athletes train hard. They do it for a gold medal that tarnishes and fades.
You're after one that's gold eternally.

1 CORINTHIANS 9:24-25 THE MESSAGE

Such a large crowd of witnesses is all around us! So we must get rid of everything that slows us down, especially the sin that just won't let go. And we must be determined to run the race that is ahead of us.

HEBREWS 12:1 CEV

My future is in your hands.
Rescue me from those who
hunt me down relentlessly.

PSALM 31:15 NLT

The strength of those who wait with hope in
the LORD will be renewed.
They will soar on wings like eagles.
They will run and won't become weary.
They will walk and won't grow tired.

ISAIAH 40:31 GOD'S WORD

It is good for me that I was afflicted,
That I may learn Your statutes.

PSALM 119:71 NASB

When you go through deep waters and
great trouble, I will be with you. When you
go through rivers of difficulty, you will not
drown! When you walk through the fire of
oppression, you will not be burned up—the
flames will not consume you.

ISAIAH 43:2 TLB

With your help I can advance
against a troop;
with my God I can scale a wall.

PSALM 18:29 NIV

Take Courage

THE MANY ROLES OF A WOMAN

You are My daughter.

Dear One,

Throughout your busy days, you pour out your love. You give so much of yourself to help your family, friends, and neighbors; and My light shines through your giving heart.

I delight in your selfless love, but know that you have yet another role—that of being rather than doing. Your greatest role of all—and one that will last throughout eternity—is that of My daughter, beloved and treasured. Rejoice in the Father who treasures you.

In perfect love,

Your Father in Heaven

> I will be a Father to you,
> and you will be my sons and daughters.
> 2 CORINTHIANS 6:18 NIV

His Holy Spirit speaks to us
deep in our hearts and tells us
that we are God's children.

ROMANS 8:16 NLT

To all who did accept him and believe in him he
gave the right to become children of God. They
did not become his children in any human way—
by any human parents or human desire. They
were born of God.

JOHN 1:12-13 NCV

What marvelous love the Father has extended to
us! Just look at it—we're called children of God!
That's who we really are. But that's also why the
world doesn't recognize us or take us seriously,
because it has no idea who he is
or what he's up to.

1 JOHN 3:1 THE MESSAGE

God's Spirit doesn't make us slaves who are
afraid of him. Instead, we become his children
and call him our Father.

ROMANS 8:15 CEV

Identity

THE SMALLEST SEED IN YOUR GARDEN

I will cause that seed to flourish.

My Precious One,

I have told you how I fashioned you
even before you were born. Now I have
something else I want to reveal to you
about your unique design. I placed a seed
of faith deep in your heart, and even before
you were aware of it, I began to tend it and
nurture it. Your heart is My garden.

Faith is not something you must strive to
grow on your own. Faith is a gift. Nurture
and protect this precious gift, and I will
cause your faith-seed to flourish. Watch
and see. It will burst forth with joy beyond
all imagining.

Faithfully yours,

The Lord Your God

"I tell you the truth, if your faith is as big as a
mustard seed, you can say to this mountain,
'Move from here to there,' and it will move.
All things will be possible for you."

MATTHEW 17:20 NCV

What is faith? It is the
confident assurance that what
we hope for is going to happen.
It is the evidence of things
we cannot yet see.

HEBREWS 11:1 NLT

Through him you believe in God who brought
Christ back to life and gave him glory. So
your faith and confidence are in God.

1 PETER 1:21 GOD'S WORD

This is a trustworthy saying that deserves full
acceptance (and for this we labor and strive),
that we have put our hope in the living God,
who is the Savior of all men,
and especially of those who believe.

1 TIMOTHY 4:9-10 NIV

God loved the people of this world so much
that he gave his only Son, so that everyone
who has faith in him will have eternal life and
never really die. God did not send his Son
into the world to condemn its people.
He sent him to save them!

JOHN 3:16-17 CEV

Faith

Faith

"Most assuredly, I say to you, he who believes in Me, the works that I do he will do also; and greater works than these he will do, because I go to My Father."

JOHN 14:12 NKJV

What does the Scripture say? "ABRAHAM BELIEVED GOD, AND IT WAS CREDITED TO HIM AS RIGHTEOUSNESS."

ROMANS 4:3 NASB

Let love and faithfulness never leave you;
bind them around your neck,
write them on the tablet of your heart.
Then you will win favor and a good name
in the sight of God and man.

PROVERBS 3:3-4 NIV

The Lord God says, See, I am placing a Foundation Stone in Zion—a firm, tested, precious Cornerstone that is safe to build on. He who believes need never run away again.

ISAIAH 28:16 TLB

Trust GOD from the bottom of your heart;
don't try to figure out everything on your own.

PROVERBS 3:5 THE MESSAGE

Then a woman who had been bleeding for twelve years came behind Jesus and touched the edge of his coat. She was thinking, "If I can just touch his clothes, I will be healed." Jesus turned and saw the woman and said, "Be encouraged, dear woman. You are made well because you believed." And the woman was healed from that moment on.

MATTHEW 9:20-22 NCV

Whatsoever ye shall ask in my name, that will I do, that the Father may be glorified in the Son. If ye shall ask any thing in my name, I will do *it*.

JOHN 14:13-14

I may have the gift to speak what God has revealed, and I may understand all mysteries and have all knowledge. I may even have enough faith to move mountains. But if I don't have love, I am nothing.

1 CORINTHIANS 13:2 GOD'S WORD

By continuing to have faith you will save your lives.

LUKE 21:19 NCV

The Smallest
Seed in
Your Garden

TAKE MY HAND

I take delight in your company.

Dearly Loved One,

Consider the delight you take in walking with a friend and enjoying your friend's conversation and companionship. Consider the sweet joy you take in observing the world through your friend's eyes. Beloved, I also take joy in your company and in your fellowship, and I long for you to take the same joy in Mine.

Come to Me. I am here. I will walk beside you every moment, listen to your thoughts and words, and delight in the knowledge that you are listening to My voice. Allow Me to be your constant companion, and you will never walk alone.

Your best Friend,

The Lord God

The LORD himself goes before you and will be with you; he will never leave you nor forsake you. Do not be afraid; do not be discouraged.

DEUTERONOMY 31:8 NIV

This is the family history of Noah. Noah was a good man, the most innocent man of his time, and he walked with God.

GENESIS 6:9 NCV

No one shall be able to stand against you all the days of your life. As I was with Moses, so I will be with you; I will not fail you or forsake you.

JOSHUA 1:5 NRSV

The LORD *is* good; his mercy *is* everlasting; and his truth *endureth* to all generations.

PSALM 100:5

"The mountains may disappear,
and the hills may come to an end,
but my love will never disappear;
my promise of peace will not come to an end,"
says the LORD who shows mercy to you.

ISAIAH 54:10 NCV

We must continue to hold firmly to our declaration of faith. The one who made the promise is faithful.

HEBREWS 10:23 GOD'S WORD

Companionship

Companionship

*God is faithful, by whom you were called into the
fellowship of His Son, Jesus Christ our Lord.*
1 CORINTHIANS 1:9 NKJV

We announce to you what we have seen and heard,
because we want you also to have fellowship with
us. Our fellowship is with God the Father and with
his Son, Jesus Christ.
1 JOHN 1:3 NCV

I led them with kindness and with love,
not with ropes.
I held them close to me; I bent down to feed them.
HOSEA 11:4 CEV

The works of his hands are faithful and just;
all his precepts are trustworthy.
They are established forever and ever,
to be performed with faithfulness and uprightness.
PSALM 111:7-8 NRSV

You make the path of life known to me.
Complete joy is in your presence.
Pleasures are by your side forever.
PSALM 16:11 GOD'S WORD

He is our God forever and ever,
and he will be our guide until we die.
PSALM 48:14 NLT

You have led the people you redeemed.
But in your lovingkindness
You have guided them wonderfully
To your holy land.

EXODUS 15:13 TLB

A person's steps are directed by the LORD,
and the LORD delights in his way.
When he falls, he will not be
thrown down headfirst
because the LORD holds on to his hand.

PSALM 37:23-24 GOD'S WORD

Even when we are too weak to have any
faith left, he remains faithful to us and will
help us, for he cannot disown us who are
part of himself, and he will always carry out
his promises to us.

2 TIMOTHY 2:13 TLB

Blessed be the Lord,
who daily bears our burden,
The God *who* is our salvation.

PSALM 68:19 NASB

Take My Hand

THE BEAUTY OF MY WORLD

Creation reflects My love.

My Own,

The world's glory reflects My beauty and My deep love for you. I designed every wildflower, every towering pine, every sunset hue, and every awesome crash of an ocean wave as a gift to refresh and delight you.

Lift your eyes to the heavens and rejoice in the spangle of stars or the first rays of the sun at daybreak. Kneel to examine a rose petal or the turn of a blade of grass ruffled by the breeze.

These are the works of My hands, beloved. Care for My world and protect it always, so that I will be glorified as the Lord of Creation.

With love,

The Creator of Heaven and Earth

Long ago you laid the foundation of the earth.
Even the heavens are the works of your hands.
PSALM 102:25 GOD'S WORD

THE HEAVENS ARE telling the glory of God; they are a marvelous display of his craftsmanship.
PSALM 19:1 TLB

You alone are the LORD. You made the heavens, even the highest heavens, and all their starry host, the earth and all that is on it, the seas and all that is in them. You give life to everything, and the multitudes of heaven worship you.
NEHEMIAH 9:6 NIV

The pastures are clothed with flocks; the valleys also are covered over with corn; they shout for joy, they also sing.
PSALM 65:13

Skies, sing for joy because the LORD
did great things!
Earth, shout for joy, even in your deepest parts!
Sing, you mountains, with thanks to God.
Sing, too, you trees in the forest!
The LORD saved the people of Jacob!
He showed his glory when he saved Israel.
ISAIAH 44:23 NCV

Nature

A Shepherd's Care

I am your Shepherd.

Beloved Daughter,

A lamb depends on its shepherd for everything: protection from danger, pastures filled with rich nourishment, and rivers of clear and flowing water.

My little one, I am your Shepherd. I will provide all your needs—even before you are aware of them. I will care for your nourishment and thirst. I will guide you to pleasant pastures where you will dwell safely with Me. If you ever lose your way, I will find you and draw you close. And, if need be, I will carry you on My shoulders.

In deepest love,

The Great Shepherd

BECAUSE THE LORD is my Shepherd, I have
everything I need!
PSALM 23:1 TLB

I am the good shepherd. The
good shepherd lays down
his life for the sheep.
JOHN 10:11 NRSV

You were like sheep that wandered away, but
now you have come back to the Shepherd and
Protector of your souls.
1 PETER 2:25 NCV

When the Chief Shepherd appears, you will
receive the crown of glory
that will never fade away.
1 PETER 5:4 NIV

O SHEPHERD OF Israel who leads Israel like a flock;
O God enthroned above the cherubim, bend
down your ear and listen as I plead. Display your
power and radiant glory.
PSALM 80:1 TLB

My God shall supply all your need according to
His riches in glory by Christ Jesus.
PHILIPPIANS 4:19 NKJV

Provision

Provision

He led forth his own people like a flock, guiding
them safely through the wilderness.

PSALM 78:52 TLB

I will fill the soul of the priests with abundance,
And My people will be satisfied with My goodness.

JEREMIAH 31:14 NASB

He gives food to those who fear him.
He remembers his agreement forever.

PSALM 111:5 NCV

By doing good, he has given evidence of his
existence. He gives you rain from heaven and crops
in their seasons. He fills you with food and your
lives with happiness.

ACTS 14:17 GOD'S WORD

Behold, the LORD's hand is not so short
That it cannot save;
Nor is His ear so dull
That it cannot hear.

ISAIAH 59:1 NASB

He tends his flock like a shepherd:
He gathers the lambs in his arms
and carries them close to his heart;
he gently leads those that have young.

ISAIAH 40:11 NIV

I'll shower blessings on the pilgrims
who come here,
and give supper to those who arrive hungry.

PSALM 132:15 THE MESSAGE

God will generously provide all you need.
Then you will always have everything you
need and plenty left over to
share with others.

2 CORINTHIANS 9:8 NLT

If your child asks you for bread, would any
of you give him a stone? Or if your child
asks for a fish, would you give him a snake?
Even though you're evil, you know how to
give good gifts to your children. So how
much more will your Father in heaven give
good things to those who ask him?

MATTHEW 7:9-11 GOD'S WORD

He will take care of the helpless and poor
when they cry to him; for they have no one
else to defend them.

PSALM 72:12 TLB

A Shepherd's
Care

GIVE ME YOUR WORRIES

Lift your eyes to Me.

Dear Precious One,

When you keep your face turned toward Mine, I will give you rest from worry and fear. Yet disheartening and troubling news sometimes causes you to look at circumstances instead of into My eyes.

The next time anxieties threaten, lift your gaze to Me. Tell Me everything that is on your heart, the worst of your dreads and fears, and the anxious thoughts that trouble you. I am here, waiting to help you, waiting to fill you with so much hope and healing that there is no room for fear. Trust Me, and see what I can do.

In My hands,

The One Who Loves You

Be strong and brave. Don't be afraid of them and don't be frightened, because the LORD your God will go with you. He will not leave you or forget you.

DEUTERONOMY 31:6 NCV

Wait for the LORD;
be strong, and let your heart
take courage;
wait for the LORD!
PSALM 27:14 NRSV

We may boldly say, The Lord *is* my helper,
and I will not fear what man shall do unto me.

HEBREWS 13:6

Don't fret or worry. Instead of worrying,
pray. Let petitions and praises shape your
worries into prayers, letting God know your
concerns. Before you know it, a sense of
God's wholeness, everything coming together
for good, will come and settle you down. It's
wonderful what happens when Christ
displaces worry at the center of your life.

PHILIPPIANS 4:6-7 THE MESSAGE

Yes, though a mighty army marches against
me, my heart shall know no fear! I am
confident that God will save me.

PSALM 27:3 TLB

I will heal this city and restore it to health. I
will heal its people, and I will give them
peace and security.

JEREMIAH 33:6 GOD'S WORD

Fear

Fear

The Spirit of the Sovereign LORD is on me,
because the LORD has anointed me
to preach good news to the poor.
He has sent me to bind up the brokenhearted,
to proclaim freedom for the captives
and release from darkness for the prisoners.
ISAIAH 61:1 NIV

This is the confidence that we have in him, that, if
we ask any thing according to his will,
he heareth us.
1 JOHN 5:14

Because GOD will be right there with you;
he'll keep you safe and sound.
PROVERBS 3:26 THE MESSAGE

Don't worry, because I am with you.
Don't be afraid, because I am your God.
I will make you strong and will help you;
I will support you with my right hand that saves you.
ISAIAH 41:10 NCV

There is no need to fear
when times of trouble come,
when enemies are surrounding me.
PSALM 49:5 NLT

Everyone who trusts the LORD
is like Mount Zion
that cannot be shaken and will stand forever.

PSALM 125:1 CEV

I have set the LORD always before me:
because *he is* at my right hand, I shall not be
moved. Therefore my heart is glad, and my
glory rejoiceth: my flesh also shall
rest in hope.

PSALM 16:8-9

People who do what is right may have
many problems,
but the LORD will solve them all.

PSALM 34:19 NCV

What do you think? With God on our side
like this, how can we lose? If God didn't
hesitate to put everything on the line for us,
embracing our condition and exposing
himself to the worst by sending his own Son,
is there anything else he wouldn't
gladly and freely do for us?

ROMANS 8:31-32
THE MESSAGE

Give Me
Your Worries

GIVE ME YOUR THOUGHTS

Open your heart and grow.

My Own,

Love Me with every fiber in your being, and with your heart, your soul, and your mind. I delight in your love when you open your heart to Me.

Consider what it means to love Me with your mind, where you think and know and understand. This kind of love requires a gradual changing of your thoughts into those that are like Mine.

Meditate on My teachings. Listen for My voice. And the qualities I love to see in My children—humbleness of heart, beauty of spirit, and wisdom beyond understanding—will be yours.

With all wisdom,

The Lord Your God

Love the Lord your God with all your heart and with all your soul and with all your mind.
MATTHEW 22:37 NIV

You will keep in perfect peace all
who trust in you,
whose thoughts
are fixed on you!
ISAIAH 26:3 NLT

The fear of the LORD is the
beginning of wisdom,
And the knowledge of the
Holy One is understanding.
PROVERBS 9:10 NASB

Are there those among you who are truly
wise and understanding? Then they should
show it by living right and doing good things
with a gentleness that comes from wisdom.
JAMES 3:13 NCV

Wisdom is like honey for your life —
if you find it, your future is bright.
PROVERBS 24:14 CEV

Reverence for the LORD is the
foundation of true wisdom.
The rewards of wisdom come
to all who obey him.
Praise his name forever!
PSALM 111:10 NLT

Transformation

An Army of Angels

I'll hold you close forever.

My Daughter,

You are surrounded by My angels. Now consider — with growing awareness and deepening peace — that there is never a moment that these glorious beings do not behold My face and await My bidding to strengthen and protect you.

All earthly things will one day pass away, but do not be fearful. Your spirit will live with Me forever. That is why I watch over your heart so carefully. Come to Me and rest secure in the presence of My angels even today. Rejoice in the safety of My arms.

Protected by Me,

The Lord Your God

Take care that you do not despise one of these little ones; for, I tell you, in heaven their angels continually see the face of my Father in heaven.

Matthew 18:10-11 NRSV

*For the Angel of the Lord
guards and rescues all who
reverence him.*
PSALM 34:7 TLB

If you make the Most High your dwelling—
even the LORD, who is my refuge—
then no harm will befall you,
no disaster will come near your tent.
For he will command his angels concerning you
to guard you in all your ways;
they will lift you up in their hands,
so that you will not strike
your foot against a stone.
PSALM 91:9-12 NIV

Behold, I am with you and will keep you
wherever you go, and will bring you back to
this land; for I will not leave you until I have
done what I have promised you.
GENESIS 28:15 NASB

The Lord is faithful; he will make you strong
and guard you from the evil one.
2 THESSALONIANS 3:3 NLT

Protection

Protection

*Behold, I send an Angel before thee, to keep thee
in the way, and to bring thee into the place which
I have prepared.*

EXODUS 23:20

When God heard the boy crying, the angel of God
called out to Hagar from heaven and said, "Hagar,
why are you worried? Don't be afraid.
I have heard your son crying."

GENESIS 21:17 CEV

He walked away, about a stone's throw, and knelt
down and prayed, "Father, if you are willing, please
take this cup of suffering away from me. Yet I want
your will, not mine." Then an angel from heaven
appeared and strengthened him.

LUKE 22:41-43 NLT

I will both lay me down in peace, and sleep: for
thou, LORD, only makest me dwell in safety.

PSALM 4:8

My presence shall go *with you*,
and I will give you rest.

EXODUS 33:14 NASB

You are my hiding place;
you will protect me from trouble
and surround me with songs of deliverance.

PSALM 32:7 NIV

Then Elisha prayed and said, "O LORD, I pray, open his eyes that he may see." And the LORD opened the servant's eyes and he saw; and behold, the mountain was full of horses and chariots of fire all around Elisha.

2 KINGS 6:17 NASB

When they suffered, he suffered also.
He sent his own angel to save them.
Because of his love and kindness,
he saved them.
Since long ago he has picked them up
and carried them.

ISAIAH 63:9 NCV

Birds find nooks and crannies in your house,
sparrows and swallows make nests there.
They lay their eggs and raise their young,
singing their songs in the place
where we worship.
GOD of the Angel Armies! King! God!
How blessed they are to live and sing there!

PSALM 84:3-4 THE MESSAGE

An Army
of Angels

In My Time, Beloved

I will give you patience.

Dear One,

You grow impatient sometimes, thinking I do not hear you when you cry out to Me. You wonder if I am listening when your prayers seem to go unanswered.

Be assured that I hear everything you think and say. Know that My timing is different from yours. I see the overall design, which is so much more than simply the here and now. I know when best to act in light of eternity. Even now I am at work in your life and in the lives of those you love.

Trust Me and be patient, beloved. My timing is perfect.

Patiently,

Your Heavenly Father

Rejoice in hope, be patient in suffering, persevere in prayer.

ROMANS 12:12 NRSV

Patience is better than strength.
Controlling your temper is
better than capturing a city.
PROVERBS 16:32 NCV

Be still in the presence of the LORD,
and wait patiently for him to act.
Don't worry about evil people who prosper
or fret about their wicked schemes.
PSALM 37:7 NLT

Whatever things were written before were
written for our learning, that we through the
patience and comfort of the Scriptures might
have hope. Now may the God of patience
and comfort grant you to be like-minded
toward one another,
according to Christ Jesus.
ROMANS 15:4-5 NKJV

I say to myself, "The LORD is my portion;
therefore I will wait for him."
The LORD is good to those
whose hope is in him,
to the one who seeks him;
it is good to wait quietly
for the salvation of the LORD.
LAMENTATIONS 3:24-26 NIV

God's Timing

THE BALM OF LAUGHTER

Rejoice with Me and laugh.

My Treasure,

At times your joy spills forth, showering everyone in your family with spontaneous laughter and song. At other times your joy is suppressed by the stresses of everyday life, financial concerns, and uncontrollable and unexpected circumstances.

During times like these, raise your eyes heavenward. Rejoice in Me, and give Me control of the challenges, trials, and triumphs of your life. Laugh with your husband and take delight in him. Sing as you go about your day, and bring smiles to the faces of those around you.

A joyful countenance can bring healing to your heart.

Joyfully,

Your Father God

A cheerful heart is a good medicine,
but a downcast spirit dries up the bones.
PROVERBS 17:22 NRSV

The statutes of the LORD are
right, rejoicing the heart:
the commandment of the Lord
is pure, enlightening the eyes.
PSALM 19:8

Let the heavens rejoice, let the earth be glad;
let the sea resound, and all that is in it;
let the fields be jubilant,
and everything in them.
Then all the trees of the forest
will sing for joy.
PSALM 96:11-12 NIV

You love what is good
And hate what is wrong.
Therefore God, your God,
Has given you more gladness
Than anyone else.
PSALM 45:7 TLB

You have endowed him with eternal blessings.
You have given him the joy of
being in your presence.
PSALM 21:6 NLT

Joy

A LIFE FILLED WITH PEACE

I satisfy your soul.

Precious Daughter,

You long for peace when things get unbearably hectic. But know, My child, that the gift of My peace is already yours.

My peace is deep and satisfying and can carry you through the most turbulent times. Accept My peace and be centered in the depths of My love and protection. Remain unshaken despite storms that may whirl around you.

Think of Me as your Fortress. No matter how the thunder rolls, the ground shakes, or the rains pound, you are safe and protected in the arms of your Heavenly Father. Let My peace begin to flood your soul right now.

Shalom,

The Prince of Peace

I truly am thirsty for you, my God.
In my heart, I am thirsty for you, the living
God. When will I see your face?
PSALM 42:1-2 CEV

There is lasting peace for those
who love your teachings.
Nothing can make
those people stumble.
PSALM 119:165 GOD'S WORD

I will hear what God the LORD will say;
For He will speak peace to His people,
to His godly ones;
But let them not turn back to folly.
PSALM 85:8 NASB

Following after the Holy Spirit leads to life
and peace, but following after the
old nature leads to death.
ROMANS 8:6 TLB

Peacemakers who sow in peace raise a
harvest of righteousness.
JAMES 3:18 NIV

Be cheerful. Keep things in good repair. Keep
your spirits up. Think in harmony. Be
agreeable. Do all that, and the God of love
and peace will be with you for sure.
2 CORINTHIANS 13:11 THE MESSAGE

All who listen to me will live in peace and
safety, unafraid of harm.
PROVERBS 1:33 NLT

God's Peace

NEVER GIVE UP

I am at work in your life.

Dear One,

I long to cradle you in My arms when I see you suffer disappointments and setbacks. You will not only make it through because of what you have endured, but you will be even stronger for it.

Without life-challenges, you would not see My grace and power at work. You would not see the unfolding of My miracles and My transforming power.

Do not give up, daughter. Know that your disappointments will strengthen you. I will transform your hardships into a triumphant crown for you to wear through all eternity.

With deepest compassion,

Your Heavenly Father

Blessed is the man who perseveres under trial, because when he has stood the test, he will receive the crown of life that God has promised to those who love him.

JAMES 1:12 NIV

Hold up my goings in thy paths, that *my footsteps slip not.*
PSALM 17:5

We're not giving up. How could we! Even though on the outside it often looks like things are falling apart on us, on the inside, where God is making new life, not a day goes by without his unfolding grace.
2 CORINTHIANS 4:16-17 THE MESSAGE

After you have suffered for a little while, the God of all grace, who has called you to his eternal glory in Christ, will himself restore, support, strengthen, and establish you.
1 PETER 5:10 NRSV

Don't get tired of doing what is good. Don't get discouraged and give up, for we will reap a harvest of blessing at the appropriate time.
GALATIANS 6:9 NLT

Those who cry as they plant crops will sing at harvest time.
PSALM 126:5 NCV

Perseverance

YOUR CHILDREN'S HERITAGE

I pour out My love on generations to come.

Beloved Daughter,

You desire to leave something of substance for your children to pass on through the generations. Some parents leave their children lands and houses, priceless antiques, or the earthly glory of an important name. But I want to tell you about a heritage with eternal value.

I will pour out glorious blessings upon the generations to follow because of your faithfulness to Me.

Earthly treasures will someday pass away, but My love and compassion will never fail—not for your children, not for your grandchildren, and not for your great-great grandchildren. What greater heritage can there be than My blessings?

With eternal love,

The Father of All

Good people live right, and God blesses the children who follow their example.

PROVERBS 20:7 CEV

Your children will grow like
a tree in the grass,
like poplar trees growing
beside streams of water.
ISAIAH 44:4 NCV

Be careful to obey all these words that I
command you today, so that it may go well
with you and with your children after you
forever, because you will be doing what is good
and right in the sight of the LORD your God.

DEUTERONOMY 12:28 NRSV

Are there those who respect the LORD?
He will point them to the best way.
They will enjoy a good life,
and their children will inherit the land.

PSALM 25:12-13 NCV

Hallelujah!
Blessed man, blessed woman, who fear GOD,
Who cherish and relish his commandments,
Their children robust on the earth,
And the homes of the upright—how blessed!
Their houses brim with wealth
And a generosity that never runs dry.

PSALM 112:1-3 THE MESSAGE

Blessings

THE BLESSINGS OF A THANKFUL HEART

I give you delight.

Dearest Child,

I delight in your thankful heart, daughter, just as you rejoice when someone hugs you in a spirit of gratitude.

When you acknowledge My gifts and wonderful blessings, you experience a sense of contentment and awe. Your heart dances with joy.

Look around you; look into the faces of those you love. Rejoice in them. Rejoice in the security of your home. Rejoice in the competence you have in your career. Count your blessings. Take delight even in the small, simple things and know that they are all from Me, beloved.

With blessings and love,

Your Heavenly Father

Sing unto the LORD, O ye saints of his, and give thanks at the remembrance of his holiness.

PSALM 30:4

Find joy in the Lord,
you righteous people.
Give thanks to him as you
remember how holy he is.
PSALM 97:12 GOD'S WORD

What I want from you is your true thanks; I
want your promises fulfilled. *I want you to*
trust me in your times of trouble, so I can
rescue you, and you can give me glory.
PSALM 50:14-15 TLB

I will give you thanks in a large gathering.
I will praise you in a crowd [of worshipers].
PSALM 35:18 GOD'S WORD

Always give thanks to God the Father for
everything, in the name of our
Lord Jesus Christ.
EPHESIANS 5:20 NCV

Praise ye the LORD. O give thanks unto the
LORD; for *he is* good: for his
mercy *endureth* for ever.
PSALM 106:1

Devote yourselves to prayer
with an alert mind and a thankful heart.
COLOSSIANS 4:2 NLT

Thanksgiving

Thanksgiving

O give thanks to the LORD, for he is good;
for his steadfast love endures forever.
1 CHRONICLES 16:34 NRSV

Through Him then, let us continually offer up a
sacrifice of praise to God, that is, the fruit of lips
that give thanks to His name.
HEBREWS 13:15 NASB

Give thanks to the LORD, call on his name;
make known among the nations what he has done.
PSALM 105:1 NIV

As you received Christ Jesus the Lord, so continue
to live in him. Keep your roots deep in him and
have your lives built on him. Be strong in the faith,
just as you were taught, and always be thankful.
COLOSSIANS 2:6-7 NCV

We must be thankful that we have a kingdom that
cannot be shaken. Because we are thankful, we must
serve God with fear and awe in a
way that pleases him.
HEBREWS 12:28 GOD'S WORD

So thank GOD for his marvelous love,
for his miracle mercy to the children he loves.
He poured great draughts of water
down parched throats;
the starved and hungry got plenty to eat.

PSALM 107:8-9 THE MESSAGE

In everything give thanks; for this is the will of
God in Christ Jesus for you.

1 THESSALONIANS 5:18 NKJV

I will give thanks to you forever
for what you have done.
In the presence of your godly people,
I will wait with hope in your good name.

PSALM 52:9 GOD'S WORD

Every created thing which is in heaven and on
the earth and under the earth and on the sea,
and all things in them, I heard saying,
"To Him who sits on the throne, and to the
Lamb, *be* blessing and honor and glory and
dominion forever and ever."

REVELATION 5:13 NASB

The Blessings of
a Thankful Heart

I CALL YOU MY FRIEND

I am your Friend forever.

Precious Friend,

I am your Heavenly Father, your God.
I am all-powerful, all-knowing, all-
compassionate, all-merciful, and eternal.
And I am your friend.

I understand your deep desire for one true
friend—someone who will always be there
for you.

I am your One True Friend. I am never too
busy or distracted to be with you. I share
your every joy and heartache. I listen to
your every need. You can talk to Me about
anything from the bottom of your heart.

With all My love,

Your Best Friend

Here I am! I stand at the door and knock. If you
hear my voice and open the door, I will come in
and eat with you, and you will eat with me.
REVELATION 3:20 NCV

Greater love has no one than this, that he lay down his life for his friends.

JOHN 15:13 NIV

Henceforth I call you not servants; for the servant knoweth not what his lord doeth: but I have called you friends; for all things that I have heard of my Father I have made known unto you.

JOHN 15:15

"If anyone loves me, they will obey me. Then my Father will love them, and we will come to them and live in them."

JOHN 14:23 CEV

I heard a loud shout from the throne, saying, "Look, the home of God is now among his people! He will live with them, and they will be his people. God himself will be with them."

REVELATION 21:3 NLT

Cast all your anxiety on him, because he cares for you.

1 PETER 5:7 NRSV

Friendship of God

THE JOY OF FRIENDSHIP

My love is a pattern for you.

Dear One,

Earthly friendship can be a reflection of My deep and abiding friendship with you. Who I am to you — My compassion, grace, wisdom, guidance, companionship, forgiveness, and joy — is a pattern for the love you give your friends. Part of My work is accomplished through your friendships.

My daughter, your friends are a precious gift from Me — planned from the moment of creation itself. Each friend is a blessing to you, and you are a blessing to each friend. Pray for one another as you weep together, laugh together, and walk together along the paths I have set before you. Be joyful in the One who brought you together.

In one accord,

The Father of All

A friend loves at all times,
and kinsfolk are born to share adversity.
PROVERBS 17:17 NRSV

Some friends play at friendship but a true friend sticks closer than one's nearest kin.

PROVERBS 18:24 NRSV

Two people are better than one,
because they get more done by
working together.
If one falls down,
the other can help him up.
But it is bad for the person
who is alone and falls,
because no one is there to help.

ECCLESIASTES 4:9-10 NCV

Love from the center of who you are; don't
fake it. Run for dear life from evil; hold on for
dear life to good. Be good friends who love
deeply; practice playing second fiddle.

ROMANS 12:9-10 THE MESSAGE

Whoever walks with wise people will be wise,
but whoever associates with fools will suffer.

PROVERBS 13:20 GOD'S WORD

It is good and pleasant
when God's people live together in peace!

PSALM 133:1 NCV

Friendship

HIDE MY WORDS IN YOUR HEART

Become more like Me.

Precious One,

I do not expect you to be perfect. It is true, beloved. Perfection can come only from Me; you cannot earn it. It is a gift that will take until eternity for you to know fully.

Your face reflects My glory; your countenance shines bright in My presence.

Draw close to Me and spend time reading My words and thinking about My promises. Begin today, beloved. Hide My words in your heart. You cannot imagine how you will grow.

With mighty plans,

Your Creator

My prayer for you is that you will overflow more and more with love for others, and at the same time keep on growing in spiritual knowledge and insight.

PHILIPPIANS 1:9 TLB

The path of the just is like the shining sun,
That shines ever brighter unto the perfect day.
PROVERBS 4:18 NKJV

We ask this so that you will live the kind of lives that prove you belong to the Lord. Then you will want to please him in every way as you grow in producing every kind of good work by this knowledge about God.

COLOSSIANS 1:10 GOD'S WORD

Don't lose a minute in building on what you've been given, complementing your basic faith with good character, spiritual understanding, alert discipline, passionate patience, reverent wonder, warm friendliness, and generous love, each dimension fitting into and developing the others.

2 PETER 1:5-7 THE MESSAGE

We all, with unveiled face, beholding as in a mirror the glory of the Lord, are being transformed into the same image from glory to glory, just as from the Lord, the Spirit.

2 CORINTHIANS 3:18 NASB

Spiritual Growth

A LIFE STITCHED TOGETHER
WITH PRAYER

I wait to hear your voice.

Beloved One,

A beautiful patchwork quilt cannot possibly hold together without stitches. So, too, your life will seem at odds and ends without prayer.

Finding time to pray in a fast-paced world is difficult. The best thing to do is to choose a time that will be the most inspiring for you. You may want to come to Me in the quiet of the morning or perhaps in the still of the night. You may want to simply pause often during the day to whisper a prayer.

I am always here, listening to your every word, whether spoken or unspoken. No matter when you choose to pray, the patterns of your days will be more restful because they will be stitched together with prayer.

Listening,

The Lord Who Loves You

Pray without ceasing.
1 THESSALONIANS 5:17

Devote yourselves to prayer,
being watchful
and thankful.

Colossians 4:2 niv

Pray in the Spirit in every situation. Use every
kind of prayer and request there is. For the
same reason be alert. Use every kind of effort
and make every kind of request for
all of God's people.

Ephesians 6:18 God's Word

What nation *is there so* great, who *hath* God
so nigh unto them, as the Lord our God *is* in
all *things that* we call upon him *for?*

Deuteronomy 4:7

If my people, who are called by my name,
will humble themselves,
pray, search for me, and turn from
their evil ways,
then I will hear [their prayer] from heaven,
forgive their sins,
and heal their country.

2 Chronicles 7:14 God's Word

Prayer

Prayer

Are you hurting? Pray. Do you feel great? Sing.
Are you sick? Call the church leaders together to
pray and anoint you with oil in the name of the
Master. Believing-prayer will heal you, and Jesus
will put you on your feet. And if you've sinned,
you'll be forgiven—healed inside and out.
JAMES 5:13-15 THE MESSAGE

The LORD hears good people when they
cry out to him,
and he saves them from all their troubles.
PSALM 34:17 NCV

When they call to me, I will answer them;
I will be with them in trouble,
I will rescue them and honor them.
With long life I will satisfy them,
and show them my salvation.
PSALM 91:15-16 NRSV

"Lord, help!" they cried, and he did! He led them
straight to safety and a place to live.
PSALM 107:6 TLB

Evening, and morning, and at noon, will I pray, and
cry aloud: and he shall hear my voice.
PSALM 55:17

Give ear to my words, O LORD,
Consider my meditation.
PSALM 5:1 NKJV

O LORD, be gracious to us;
we long for you.
Be our strength every morning,
our salvation in time of distress.

ISAIAH 33:2 NIV

You listen to the longings
of those who suffer.
You offer them hope,
and you pay attention to their cries for help.

PSALM 10:17 CEV

O Lord, listen to my prayers; give me the
common sense you promised.

PSALM 119:169 TLB

As they listen, their secret thoughts will be
laid bare, and they will fall down on their
knees and worship God, declaring,
"God is really here among you."

1 CORINTHIANS 14:25 NLT

Come, kneel before the Lord our Maker.

PSALM 95:6 TLB

A Life Stitched
Together with
Prayer

THE PROMISE OF ETERNITY

You will live with Me forever.

Precious Daughter,

I have written to you about My wondrous gifts of grace and peace and beauty and joy. These gifts express My abundant love for you.

The cost of My greatest gift to you was dear. My Son paid for it by laying down His life for you. He conquered death, once and for all, to bring you the gift of living with Me forever.

I will someday welcome you to the home I have prepared for you. You will look joyfully into My face, My cherished one, and see at last the splendid depths of My love for you.

Forever yours in love,

The God of All Eternity

> In my Father's house are many rooms; if it were not so, I would have told you. I am going there to prepare a place for you.
>
> JOHN 14:2 NIV

This is the testimony in essence:
God gave us eternal life;
the life is in his Son.
1 JOHN 5:11 THE MESSAGE

I am the Alpha and the Omega, the First and
the Last, the Beginning and the End.
REVELATION 22:13 NLT

They will hunger no more,
and thirst no more;
the sun will not strike them,
nor any scorching heat;
for the Lamb at the center of the throne
will be their shepherd,
and he will guide them to springs
of the water of life,
and God will wipe away every tear
from their eyes.
REVELATION 7:16-17 NRSV

We know that if the life we live here on
earth is ever taken down like a tent, we still
have a building from God. It is an eternal
house in heaven that isn't made by
human hands.
2 CORINTHIANS 5:1 GOD'S WORD

Heaven

Heaven

God shall wipe away all tears from their eyes;
and there shall be no more death, neither sorrow,
nor crying, neither shall there be any more pain:
for the former things are passed away.
REVELATION 21:4

A river of fire was flowing
from in front of him.
Many thousands of angels were serving him,
and millions of angels stood before him.
Court was ready to begin,
and the books were opened.
DANIEL 7:10 NCV

After this I looked and there before me was a great
multitude that no one could count, from every
nation, tribe, people and language, standing before
the throne and in front of the Lamb. They were
wearing white robes and were holding palm
branches in their hands.
REVELATION 7:9 NIV

Our citizenship is in heaven. And we eagerly await a
Savior from there, the Lord Jesus Christ.
PHILIPPIANS 3:20 NIV

Keep yourselves in the love of God, looking for the
mercy of our Lord Jesus Christ unto eternal life.
JUDE 21

Your eyes will see the King in His beauty;
They will see the land that is very far off.

ISAIAH 33:17 NKJV

I heard again what sounded like the shouting
of a huge crowd, or like the waves of a
hundred oceans crashing on the shore, or
like the mighty rolling of great thunder,
"Praise the Lord. For the Lord our God,
the Almighty, reigns."

REVELATION 19:6 TLB

I tell you the truth, whoever hears my word
and believes him who sent me has eternal
life and will not be condemned; he has
crossed over from death to life.

JOHN 5:24 NIV

Friends, confirm God's invitation to you, his
choice of you. Don't put it off; do it now.
Do this, and you'll have your life on a firm
footing, the streets paved and the way wide
open into the eternal kingdom of our Master
and Savior, Jesus Christ.

2 PETER 1:10-11 THE MESSAGE

The Promise
of Eternity

187

The Faithful Promises of God

Live under the protection of God Most High and stay in the shadow of God All-Powerful.
PSALM 91:1 CEV

The LORD will guide you continually,
And satisfy your soul in drought,
And strengthen your bones;
You shall be like a watered garden,
And like a spring of water,
whose waters do not fail.
Isaiah 58:11 NKJV

The meek shall eat and be satisfied;
They shall praise the LORD that seek him;
Your heart shall live for ever.
PSALM 22:26

His divine power has given us everything needed for
life and godliness, through the knowledge of him
who called us by his own glory and goodness.
2 PETER 1:3 NRSV

Great is our LORD, and of great power: his
understanding is infinite.

PSALM 147:5

Those who walked in the dark have seen a
bright light. And it shines upon everyone
who lives in the land of darkest shadows.

ISAIAH 9:2 CEV

Let us therefore draw near with confidence
to the throne of grace, that we may receive
mercy and may find grace to help in
time of need.

HEBREWS 4:16 NASB

I will refresh the weary and satisfy the faint.

JEREMIAH 31:25 NIV

Give your burdens to the LORD, and he will
take care of you. He will not permit the
godly to slip and fall.

PSALM 55:22 NLT

Thank You, God

If you have enjoyed this book, we invite
you to visit our website to learn about
other Harvest House books and products:

www.harvesthousepublishers.com

HARVEST HOUSE PUBLISHERS

EUGENE, OREGON